BUYING MAINTAINING A MODERN TRADITIONAL MORGAN

BUYING AND MAINTAINING A MODERN TRADITIONAL MORGAN

DAVID WELLINGS

Foreword by Steve Morris

THE CROWOOD PRESS

First published in 2018 by
The Crowood Press Ltd
Ramsbury, Marlborough
Wiltshire SN8 2HR

enquiries@crowood.com

www.crowood.com

This impression 2020

British Library Cataloguing-in-Publication Data
A catalogue record for this book is available from the British Library.

ISBN 978 1 78500 377 6

Disclaimer
Safety is of the utmost importance in every aspect of an automotive
workshop. The practical procedures and the tools and equipment
used in automotive workshops are potentially dangerous. Tools should
be used in strict accordance with the manufacturer's recommended
procedures and current health and safety regulations. The author
and publisher cannot accept responsibility for any accident or injury
caused by following the advice given in this book.

Designed and typeset by Guy Croton Publishing Services,
Maidstone, Kent
Printed and bound in India by Replika Press Pvt Ltd

CONTENTS

ACKNOWLEDGEMENTS

This book would not have been possible without the following:

My wife Margaret and daughter Jayne, for putting up with a car fanatic in the house for so many years, with so much patience and tolerance. And mugs of tea!

My two 'willing volunteer' proof readers, Simon Hall and John Stride, and all those Morgan enthusiasts who frequent *Talk Morgan* on-line, and have welcomed and encouraged my ramblings since 2008. Also very special thanks to Simon Murphy, who founded the *Talk Morgan* forum, and also Brian Voakes, and Keith Jackson at Brands Hatch Morgans for their invaluable assistance.

All those officers and members of the Morgan Sports Car Club, who have made such encouraging noises about my monthly 'Concours Spot' in *Miscellany* over the last six years.

Steve Morris, managing director of Morgan Motor Co., for agreeing to contribute the Foreword, and especially to all the people who work at Morgan Motor Company: for what they build, for the unique experience their cars provide on the road, for the magical experience provided on factory tours, and their personal involvement with customers who take the plunge on a new build.

Finally, my grateful thanks to Richard Palmer, a Morgan enthusiast who lives in Australia, who sent me a copy of the Dealer Notice from Morgan Motor Company, dated 3 July 1997. The title is 'June 1997 Bodywork Revisions', and six pages from this notice are reproduced at Appendix II.

All photographs are by the author unless otherwise credited to the following: Glenn Barker; Jochen Ernsting; Roger Gates; Peter Gilbert; Steve Harris; John Hayes; Steve Langston; Dirk Mattheus; Richard Palmer; Adrian Slade; John Stride.

FOREWORD

Morgan history is steeped in examples of sheer dedication as demonstrated by the individuals, companies and bodies of people who have collaborated with Morgan in a quest to create a luxury vehicle, or an associated Morgan-related product or service, which will, quite literally, put a smile on the user's face from the day they collect their vehicle. Their aim is to create a unique, total experience which ensures that customers create a special bond with their vehicles.

If one word could describe the Morgan story it would be evolution, because since the birth of the company in 1909 we have been fortunate in witnessing an ever-increasing global customer base, people who own, maintain and add to their Morgan stable, which for any marque is a testament to both vehicles and customers. More importantly for Morgan, this demonstrates the value of our cars to their owners, and the longevity of ownership – in some instances more than forty years – clearly places further emphasis on the importance of vehicle maintenance.

Because of this unique customer/ownership model, the maintenance of their vehicles has, and remains, an extremely important part of the overall Morgan experience. This book helps to describe this crucial and intrinsic facet of their journey.

Morgan is now in its 108th year of vehicle manufacture, and reliable sources indicate that in excess of 90 per cent of all four-wheeled Morgan cars are still on the road, or in existence in some form or another. It is therefore even more important that the knowledge and practical experience contained within this book has now been made available for owners to reference throughout their vehicle/ownership lifecycle.

It is often quoted that every Morgan is bespoke and entirely individual, and this is very often an important factor in customer satisfaction, particularly because this element of ownership adds to the experience at the ever-increasing number of Morgan gatherings and events. This unique Morgan experience is further enhanced by the significant variety of vehicle options and after-market accessories that are available. It is widely acknowledged that this, in addition to the evolution of the model range throughout our history, has ensured that each customer can create their own unique and individual car to suit their personal taste and requirements.

An intrinsic part of the Morgan story are those owners and enthusiasts such as David Wellings, who are tremendous ambassadors for the marque. They ensure that both existing and new customers are welcomed and have the opportunity to access vital expertise, knowledge and statistics pertinent to the model range. This gives an extremely useful platform both for the existing customer base, and to those who are considering buying their first Morgan.

The traditional Morgan story and model evolution has been exciting, and is extremely interesting when looking back. The company heritage has been well documented in a variety of sources over the years. It is certainly timely for a publication of this nature, with the 4/4 now in its eighty-first year of production – which as a company we are proud to say, makes it the longest-running production vehicle model in the world.

This book is a truly valuable addition to the Morgan knowledge base, and exemplifies the embodiment of the Morgan community spirit, demonstrating how individuals strive to add value to the Morgan experience for the wider Morgan audience. I would personally like to thank David Wellings and the contributors to this book, for their valuable effort in ensuring the traditional Morgan continues to thrive, and remains operational through good maintenance and the knowledge acquired through shared experiences.

Unquestionably the production of this book has been a huge undertaking, involving a significant amount of work, time and effort to collect and collate information of this nature, and I have absolutely no doubt that all Morgan owners and the Morgan community as a whole will be extremely grateful to the author David Wellings.

Steve Morris
Managing Director
Morgan Motor Company Ltd

INTRODUCTION

I joined the Morgan Sports Car Club in 2003 after many years of living and breathing MG cars. I had reached the point where I could consider fulfilling a dream of buying a Morgan. My previous experiences of the MG Owners Club and MG Car Club had shown clearly that marque-specific car clubs provide an invaluable resource, and a huge amount of information and pool of knowledge to both potential and new owners. I wished to take full advantage of this expertise, before taking the plunge into my first Morgan. This cautious approach also gave me a five-year lead-in, during which time I hoped to convince my wife that my plan was a good idea.

In the summer of 2008 I had visited my nearest Morgan dealer, where I was made very welcome, and I had a short test drive in a 2005 Roadster, courtesy of a very considerate and generous regular customer. I had also arranged a ride out in an older Morgan Plus 8 with a local MSCC member, so I could make a direct comparison with the MGBGTV8 which I owned at that time. All of this confirmed to me that I was doing the right thing.

It didn't take long to sell my MGB, in July 2008, and this happened rather sooner than my wife or I had expected. Earlier in the year, my first step had been to create a list of the optional extras which I thought I would like to have when buying a Morgan. This list was based on my acquired knowledge from reading *Miscellany*, the monthly magazine of the Morgan Sports Car Club, over the previous five years. I had also researched various Morgan-related websites at length.

By July 2008, I believed that I had enough of the detail clear in my mind – but the reality was very different. In truth, I only had some of the information that I really needed to buy the right Morgan. Despite

this handicap, I did manage to locate and buy the car that I really wanted, but a lot of luck was involved! I had been scoping the classifieds for some time, and at the end of August 2008 I drove home from a village near Telford along the A5 and A38, on a fine, dry summer's day, soaking up my first real Morgan experience in a 2005 3-litre V6 Roadster.

The Morgan Roadster was not part of my initial thinking, because I had intended to seek out a classic Morgan Plus 8, after driving behind the Rover V8 engine in my MGB for the previous twenty-two years. But they do say that a Morgan will choose you, and this Roadster literally took my breath away. It looked spectacular in Corsa Red with a black interior, black carpets edged in red, stainless wire wheels, and an easy-up hood. It was just three years old, and with around 5,000 miles recorded. The fact that it had first been a dealer demonstrator, and had already had two owners subsequently, did not put me off! With the benefit of eight years' experience, and a dash of hindsight, I now realize that I went into this adventure quite ill informed, despite trying to get to grips with the intricacies of Morgan cars over the previous five years.

My experiences in buying my first Morgan, and in maintaining and improving it, became the catalyst for this book. Despite there being a wide and interesting selection of Morgan books on the market, none provide a layman's ownership guide to the modern traditional four-wheeled Morgan. Towards the end of 2008 I discovered *Talk Morgan*, an on-line forum of Morgan enthusiasts, and it wasn't long before I was posting my 'taking care of things' efforts on to this forum, something which has continued to this day.

In 2013 we decided to expand our fleet, and added a 2-litre Morgan 4/4 75th Anniversary to our collection. Again, this Morgan chose us, and with 12,000 miles already recorded in twelve months, provided even more opportunities to take care of things. We enjoyed this Morgan for three years, and had some fantastic touring holidays in it. Then in the spring of 2016, we decided to push the boat out, and order a new Morgan Plus 4, so that we could enjoy the full new car factory experience. This time I knew exactly what I wanted! Our car went through the factory in June 2016 and I was present to watch the build whenever I could get down there. We were not disappointed with the result.

The author, plus 2005 Series I V6 3-litre Roadster.

In 2010 I became Concours Secretary for the Morgan Sports Car Club, and I held this position until the AGM in April 2017, when I stood down. In that role I organized the annual concours event, and wrote a monthly column, 'The Concours Spot', in *Miscellany*, the magazine of the MSCC. Of necessity, my brief extended beyond pure concours matters, and some of the Morgan improvements and maintenance tips which featured there, are incorporated in this book. Over the past eight years I was often asked why I didn't compile my ownership experiences into a book. For all the usual reasons, but mainly due to lack of time, this didn't happen until 'now', when my New Year resolution finally took hold, and the writing began in January 2017.

In the context of this book title I would like to set the scene, and explain how my definition of a modern traditional Morgan came about. My own experiences have related to a conventional steel chassis car with aluminium panels, Superform wings, and a stainless-steel bulkhead. This definition, and therefore this book, doesn't include the Aero range, or Aero-based Plus 8, although the chapters on the body tub and hood are equally relevant to the current Aero Plus 8.

For those readers who may not be too familiar with the evolution of the traditional Morgan, I will add a little more detail. To the untrained eye, a Morgan is a Morgan, and they all look the same. Well, they do from a distance. But the reality is very different when you look more closely. The traditional shape, which has survived for so long, actually hides a huge number of evolutionary changes. It is not my intention to ignore the four-seater variant, and most of my writing will relate equally to the four-seater, but my personal experience is wholly based on the two-seater Morgan. The pivotal moment in the evolution of the modern traditional Morgan arrived in 1997, and I will explain more about this in Chapter 1.

Within the Morgan Sports Car Club is an active group of owners who race, hillclimb and sprint their modern traditional Morgans. Using a Morgan in this way is outside the scope of my experiences, and this book. I will admit though, to having driven up the hill at Prescott and Shelsley Walsh, and enjoyed these experiences! There is a huge range of competition information available from the MSCC, and from a number of dealers and specialists who are long-standing and highly experienced Morgan competitors, if you wish to participate in these activities.

CHAPTER ONE

BUYING A MODERN TRADITIONAL MORGAN

The pivotal moment in Morgan history, which became the genesis of the modern traditional Morgan, arrived in 1997. It was during this year that the Morgan Motor Company made a huge investment into commissioning Superform wings.

This process is where sheet aluminium is heated to a plastic state, and then moulded over a former, using air pressure. Morgan Motor Co. have informed me that the Superform wings were originally CAD designed and tooled from three sets of Morgan 4/4 hand-fabricated wings, so when they were first test fitted in wider form to the Plus 8, some additional shaping was needed to get a good fit. It was also the intention to wire roll the edges in order to maintain the look of the earlier hand-made wings, but this was found to be impossible due to the inherent stiffness in the Superform structure. This is why the U channel edge finishing profile was introduced.

It was around this time that the Plus 8 was at its widest, due to a batch of 7in-wide wire wheels being fitted as an option, and for a while the headlamp bowls were shifted inwards slightly to balance the gap to the cowl.

The 1997 (1998 model year) sales brochure covers some of these changes:

The new cars feature one-piece front wings manufactured using superformed (SPF) aluminium. The result is a superior lightweight wing with improved strength and corrosion resistance. Stainless-steel exhausts are now fitted as standard on all cars. The front wing valances, bulkhead, and front and rear bumpers are now manufactured in stainless steel for strength and durability.

In addition, a revised side-impact scuttle bar was fitted as standard behind the A posts.

In order to offer airbags as an option, the cockpit area was redesigned, moving the occupants back slightly, moving the scuttle forwards slightly, and adding a couple of inches to the doors – hence the term 'long door' and 'short door'. At the same time, the Salisbury rear axle was replaced with the Australian BTR unit. These changes were announced mid-year, and would therefore have fed through into production later in 1997. However, a very important point to note is that although the body tub revisions were notified to dealers in June 1997, this update does not mention the Superform wings or stainless-steel bulkhead. Recollection at the factory is that the wings and bulkhead changes came later in that year, around October.

So we can now understand that 1997 was a year of radical change which progressed from June. Any Morgan built after June in that year is likely to show some signs of these changes; thus any Morgan built between June and October may well be a long door car with a steel bulkhead and hand-formed rolled-edge wings. Only the cars built after October are likely to feature all these enhancements.

My definition of the modern traditional Morgan therefore very conveniently spans the period from 1997 to the present day, and so is 'twenty years of the modern traditional Morgan'! Thousands of books have been written about cars, and in most cases, if the author digs deep enough and speaks with the right people, the facts and the detail will emerge. But Morgan isn't really like this, because there is no production line: order numbers are not necessarily commissioned into production in numerical order, and chassis numbers are not necessarily built in order.

My first Morgan, a 2005 Roadster, as viewed for the first time on 23 August 2008.

Therefore the usual basis for establishing change points in production doesn't apply. On a working day in Malvern, a box of parts from the stores, with a build book, is paired with a chassis. So for example, on the day the brake calipers were changed from Lockheed to Caparo, cars could have been built with either type of caliper, and it would bear no relationship to either the order number or the chassis number.

With that in mind, when I mention change points, it must always be regarded as indicative and approximate. Not only that, but change points are never at 31 December, and so when a year for a change point is noted, all we can know for certain is that the change probably happened sometime during that year.

THE NEW OPTIONS

There is a comprehensive and wide-ranging list of optional extras which your dealer will be happy to provide, and which is also available on line on the Morgan Motor Co. website. There is also a 'car creator' function on the Morgan website, and this will allow you to build your ideal virtual Morgan.

If you are fortunate enough to be able to order a new Morgan, then relish every moment of the process, from when you first visit your chosen dealer, to when you take delivery of your new Morgan. If at all possible, you should try to visit the factory at Malvern Link as often as possible during the seventeen-day build, and make the most of an incredible, probably unique car-buying experience. Your dealer will advise you when the build commences, and your car will make rapid progress through the factory. A photo-build record is available on the new options list, and you should give this very serious consideration, because it adds greatly to the overall experience.

If you are looking at a used Morgan, then begin your search by scrutinizing the new options list. Every Morgan is different, and you may find a used car which has up to £10,000 of optional extras. That additional cost new won't necessarily translate into the secondhand asking price, and two used Morgans at similar prices may have had significantly different prices when new. Don't rule out a private purchase, either. I fully expected to buy my first Morgan at a Morgan dealer, with all the security and reassurance

Production Numbers

This subject is really quite difficult to research and establish the facts. We know that the factory produce somewhere in the region of 750 to 850 Morgans each year. Within that number from 2002 has been the Aero8 and derivatives, and from 2012, the Morgan three-wheeler. The Morgan 4/4 has always tended to be the most popular model, and therefore built in greater numbers. Since 1997, from the information which is available, we can deduce that around 200 4/4s have been built each year, making a total number of over 4,000 cars since 1997.

The Morgan Plus 4 has been built in smaller numbers, and the evidence suggests that around 750 were built from 1997 with the Rover T16 engine, up to the year 2000. The Duratec-engined Plus 4 seems to be closer to 1,000 units up to 2012, and the GDI, which remains in production, stands at over 200 units. The Morgan Plus 8 was built in similar numbers to the Plus 4 in the period up to 2004, although production increased towards the end, when its demise became public knowledge. We can therefore deduce that around 1,300 Plus 8s were built in long-door form.

Finally the Morgan Roadster. With so many versions in such a short period of time means that without knowing the exact month of change we can only estimate the numbers of each. The evidence suggests around 600 Series 1 Roadsters, 300 Series 2, and 600 Series 3, making just short of 1,500 units up to 2012. It appears that the 3.7 Roadster has not met the numbers achieved by the earlier models, and that somewhere in the region of 400 have been produced at the time of writing. Around 80 per cent of production is exported, and this means that UK-specification cars across this period are only available in very small numbers. The Morganville Registry (www.Morganville. org) contains some valuable data on production numbers, and an owners' register of Morgan cars.

that this brings, but I did the unexpected in buying privately, without regret (the usual buyer's precautions apply when doing this).

THE MODEL RANGE 1997–2017

There are only three models in the modern traditional Morgan range: the 4/4, the Plus 4, and the Roadster (which replaced the classic Plus 8 in 2004).

THE MORGAN 4/4

By 1997, the Morgan 4/4 was fitted with the 1796cc Ford Zetec engine. The Zetec Silver Top 4/4s were built up to 1999 with a Gemmer steering box, but with an option of a Jack Knight steering rack. The Silver Top continued to 2002 with a steering rack as standard, and with a quick rack option (three turns lock to lock) to match the light weight and agile handling of the 4/4. The Zetec Black Top replaced the Silver Top in 2002 and was built until 2005, when the Zetec unit was replaced with the 1798cc Ford Duratec engine, with a small increase in power, from around 111bhp to 125bhp. Around the same time, a Quaife steering rack was fitted with three and a half turns lock to lock.

In addition, in 2003, Morgan had launched a new entry level model, the Runabout, which was based on the 4/4. The Runabout had a reduced number of bonnet louvres, and this model came in three standard colours with a fairly basic specification. The colours chosen were red, white and blue, these being Regal red, Whitehall white, and Bulldog blue. Obviously very patriotic! I have seen a silver Runabout, which indicates that a special paint order may have been allowed.

In 2008, the 1800cc Duratec engine was replaced with the 1600cc Ford Sigma engine in the 4/4, which was initially built only in Sport specification. This engine delivers 110bhp, and loves to be driven hard. The Sport model came with no spare wheel and with a track pack option, which included a competition roll hoop, and four-point racing harnesses. The philosophy of a limited colour palette, and limited bespoke options from the Runabout, was continued into the 4/4 Sport production run. As the factory

This might be 'any model', as the wings are not yet fitted. The factory use slave wheels to move cars around, and here there are two Plus 4 wheels and a Roadster wheel. Only the engine gives the game away. This is a Plus 4, and the body tub has just been fitted to the chassis. The roll hoop which fits under the scuttle is visible on the floor under the rear axle; this will be fitted next.

concentrated on 4/4 Sport production, for a while there were no bespoke 4/4s. Eventually the Sport specification was incorporated into the relaunched bespoke options list for the Morgan 4/4. The 4/4 used the Ford MT-75 five-speed gearbox until 2012, when it was replaced with the Mazda MX5 five-speed unit. It would be logical to assume that the introduction of the Sigma engine in the Morgan 4/4 coincided with the introduction of the Sport model. This was not so, and of course we know that Morgan production is not so predictable. Factory sources have confirmed that there had been twenty-four RHD and twenty-five LHD Sigma-engined bespoke 4/4s before the introduction of the 4/4 Sport model. These early Sigma engine-4/4s also came with thin rear reflectors mounted under the edge of the rear wings and wing-top mounted sidelights, and of course a spare wheel. Delivery of the 4/4s with the new engine was delayed, until readings from the new ECU were passed by the DoT.

THE MORGAN PLUS 4

In 1997, the Morgan Plus 4 was fitted with the 2-litre Rover T16 engine, and Rover R380 five-speed gearbox. This model lasted in production until 2000, when the Plus 4 temporarily ceased production. After a four-year break the Morgan Plus 4 was reintroduced, and was fitted with the 2-litre Ford Duratec engine with the Ford MT-75 five-speed gearbox. This proved to be a very successful and popular package, and this model survived until the Geneva motor show in 2014, when the Plus 4 GDI was announced, with 154bhp and 148lb/ft of torque, which was a small increase over the 145bhp and 138lb/ft of torque of the previous Duratec model. In 2012 the Plus 4 was fitted with the Mazda MX5 five-speed gearbox.

A limited number of Plus 4 Sport models have been built, and a limited number of narrow-bodied Plus 4s, which were initially launched as the '4/4 75th Anniversary' cars. This model had Plus 4 running gear in a 4/4 package, with narrow wings and wheels, and with 185/70 Avon performance tyres. Three standard colours were available – Sport black, Sport red, and Old English white. One car was finished in Sport yellow to special order. There have been three high performance versions of the Plus 4 in this period, all of which were produced in limited numbers with very limited bespoke options. These are the Plus 4 Super Sport, the Plus 4 Baby Doll (a competition car), and the Aero Racing Plus 4 (ARP4). In 2018 at the Geneva Motor Show, Morgan announced a new development of the Plus 4. The Morgan Plus 4 'Club

Sport' was announced as an entry level race car, ideal for those looking to start racing, sprinting or hill climbing, but also road legal. This model comes with a choice of 4 Club Sport colours with contrasting graphics. The upgrades from the standard Plus 4 are as follows; The engine ECU is re-mapped and a revised sports exhaust system produces 180bhp at the flywheel. An oil cooler is fitted. The suspension is modified with a Panhard rod, and four externally adjustable dampers. The brakes have competition pads, race specification brake fluid, and a brake bias valve. Wheels are four 6.5 × 15 bolt-on alloys. There is no spare wheel.

THE FOUR-SEATERS

Towards the end of 1996, the 4/4 four-seater was built with a rear bench seat. A change in safety regulations overtook this design, and it wasn't until 1999 that a redesigned twin rear bucket seat was made available in the long-door body tub, and the 4/4 four-seater restarted production. But this was only until 2003, when once again the four-seater was discontinued. The four-seater was relaunched at the end of 2005, and exhibited at Geneva in 2006 as a Roadster, with a Plus 4 four-seater also available. The design now had curved rear sidescreens, a redesigned rear body section, and a much improved hood design. These models continued in production to November 2016, but were only built in very limited numbers.

THE MORGAN PLUS 8

In 1997, the traditional Morgan Plus 8 was available with the Rover V8 engine, of either 3.9 litres (some were marketed as 4.0 litres), or 4.6 litres with the Rover R380 five-speed gearbox. The GEMS (Land Rover) 3.9-litre V8 produced 190bhp, and the 4.6-litre produced 194.4bhp. The real difference was in the torque – 225lb/ft vs 260lb/ft. The Morgan Plus 8 was never offered with the four-seater bodywork, although two four-seater Plus 8s are known to exist.

THE MORGAN ROADSTER

In 2004, the Rover V8 engine was replaced with the Ford 3-litre V6 Duratec engine, and renamed 'Roadster'. Retrospectively this model became the Series 1 Roadster, and the Ford Mondeo ST220-derived V6 produced 223bhp, and 200lb/ft of torque. The initial engineering on this unit came from Porsche, who were also developing a V6 engine, and Cosworth, who helped with cylinder-head manufacturing. The Series 1 Roadster has a Getrag 221 five-speed gearbox with direct drive in fifth, and used a 3.08:1 rear-axle ratio.

A limited number of lightweight Roadsters was built, and these were aimed at competition use. They were fitted with bolt-on alloy wheels and were stripped out inside. These cars were usually two-tone, and most appear to have been built with a dark blue body and silver wings, and with a hardtop, although other colours were also produced.

The revised Series 2 and Series 3 production Roadsters have the Ford MT-75 five-speed gearbox with direct drive in fourth, an overdrive fifth, and with a 3.73:1 axle ratio. The overall gearing is almost the same, but the later Roadsters are very slightly higher geared overall in fifth gear. These later Roadsters were powered by a Ford Escape-derived 3-litre V6, which is closely related to the earlier V6, and which was fitted to a range of small SUVs in the United States.

The S2 Roadster specification engine delivered 201bhp, and was adopted by Morgan from around 2007 to 2010. In 2007, this engine had been significantly reworked by Ford, releasing 240bhp, and 223lb/ft of torque. This engine was adopted by Morgan in 2010, into what became the S3 Roadster, and a Roadster Sport option was introduced at the same time. Finally, in 2013, after a short break in Roadster production, this V6 engine was replaced with the Ford 3.7-litre V6 Cyclone engine used in the Mustang, and the power increased to 280bhp. This model is fitted with the Ford/Getrag MT-82 six-speed gearbox.

In 2015 the first customer Morgan Aero Racing V6 (ARV6) was produced: this model is a hard-core competition car, based on the 3.7-litre Roadster, and has been built in extremely limited numbers. At the Geneva Motor Show in 2006, the new Roadster four-seater was exhibited, and this model was available until November 2016. At the Geneva Motor Show in 2018, Morgan announced that from April 2018, the

Note here the narrow gap between headlamp nacelle and cowl of a Morgan 4/4.

The wider gap of the 2005 Roadster. In 2010, the Plus 4 and Roadster received a wider front frame (crosshead), so the more recent Plus 4 has a gap similar to this, whilst the later Roadsters have a wider gap. Note also the different position of the indicator lamp relative to the headlamp.

Roadster would be built with the five-link rear suspension, previously used in the limited edition ARP4. Rear disc brakes would become an aero Racing option at extra cost.

BODY WIDTH

All modern traditional Morgans now share a common chassis and body tub width. This means that any of the current traditional models will provide the same amount of interior space 'door to door'. However, the 3.7-litre Roadster has a larger gearbox than the earlier 3-litre Roadsters, and current 4-cylinder cars. This means that the transmission tunnel is wider, thus making the footwells narrower, although a small amount of extra space has been found in the outer bulkhead panels on these cars.

The dimensional differences between each model in the traditional range are simply to be found in the width of the wings. These all begin the same size, but are expertly trimmed along the inside edges to fit each car, and to accommodate the different width of wheels and tyres that are available for each model. This can be observed in two places. The width across the rear wing, from the body tub beading to the wing edge, varies by model. The distance between the edge of the radiator cowl and the headlamp nacelle also varies according to model. The Morgan 4/4 has less than 20mm (1in) width between the cowl and headlamp nacelle, whereas the Roadster reveals a significantly larger distance – about 80mm (4in) – between the two. The Plus 4, as you might expect, is somewhere in between. Note also that the headlamp nacelles of the modern traditional Morgan are placed slightly further out on the wings than they were on the cars built before 1997.

ABOVE: *A short-door car, without door handles, which were an option at that time. In 2017 door handles are standard, with a delete option at extra cost. Also evident here is the distinct narrowing of the bulkhead above the upper hinge.* RICHARD PALMER

Long-Door Cars

The doors gained approximately 50mm (2in) in length when airbags became an option in 1997 (these were later discontinued), and the bulkhead was moved forwards. At the same time the windscreen demister vents were discontinued, and an electrically heated screen was introduced. And so the heated front screen cars are long-door cars.

It is very easy to spot a long-door car: simply compare the distance between the trailing edge of the door and the beading where the rear wing meets the body, and the long door/shorter gap is apparent. Longer doors make getting in and out easier, so if you are taller, then a long-door car may be the better option for you. Remember also that two different door lengths result in two sets of sidescreen dimensions, and the sidescreen shape and seal design has also evolved over time.

Early Morgans in this period, which had the flat composite A pillars, also had sidescreen frames with a rubber seal on the front edge, along the top, and down the trailing edge. This is yet one more reason why Morgans can look so very different from each other. There was a further alteration to the sidescreen trim panel around 2010, when the trailing edge was straightened. Originally the shape was concave to match up with the curve of the rear wheel arch.

There is a factory option available on the doors, of elasticated pockets, which may also have a contrasting colour top edge; there is also a leather trim option on the steering column surround, and also around the interior door locks. When this option is not specified, the steering column surround and door-lock covers are black plastic.

OPPOSITE: *A long-door car, with door handles. Compare this to the previous image and you will note the reduced gap between the door and wing, and the wider bulkhead panel above the upper hinge. Note also the shaped lower profile of the sidescreen panel, and compare this with the next image.*

Some Morgans are distinctly lozenge shaped, in that the rear track may be almost 150mm (6in) wider than the front track. This becomes very important if you have limited access into your garage. Wire wheels provide a slightly wider track than bolt-on alloy wheels of the same width, and there have been two widths of front crossheads fitted (the front tubular frame). Initially, in the period covered by this book, the crosshead on all models, measured between the bottom of the kingpins, was 1,030mm (40.5in); in 2010 this was widened for the Plus 4 and S3 Roadster, to 1,110mm (43.75in). The 4/4 model has continued with the narrower crosshead.

By searching the dealer websites and classifieds you will also find that there are bespoke Plus 4s with 4/4 wheels, and bespoke Plus 4s with Roadster wheels. No two cars are exactly the same, and it's very much down to personal choice as to which combination you find most attractive to look at, and live with. Some enthusiasts prefer the narrow front aspect of the 4/4, and this includes the 'narrow Plus 4'.

HOOD TYPES AND MATERIALS

There is a simple choice of hood material: either Everflex (vinyl), or mohair (Twillfast). The standard colour is black, but there are many other colour options available, usually at extra cost.

THE TRADITIONAL HOOD

This hood type fits over the windscreen header rail using nine lift-the-dot fasteners, and fits on to the rear tub with a mixture of lift-the-dot, durable dot and turnbuckle fasteners. Note that 'turnbuckle' has become the accepted and recognized name for a fastener which is more properly known as a 'turn-button' fastener. I will use the accepted name of 'turnbuckle' in this book.

The studded hood type has three rear window panels in plastic, and this hood can be removed completely when not in use. It gives the Morgan a very clean profile when tucked away, but leaves the area behind the seats exposed, unless a tonneau cover is used. Where a tonneau cover was not specified from new, the Morgan won't be fitted with tonneau

A traditional Everflex hood. Three turnbuckle fasteners are visible on the B panel to the rear of the door; the traditional hood overlaps the edge of the B-post panel.

cover attachments to the body tub. This means that in order to retro fit the lift-the-dot studs on to the bulkhead, the windscreen will probably need removing to provide sufficient access for drilling, and is a job probably best left to the experts. This hood type attaches to the frame using Velcro tubes.

The A posts or pillars that secure the windscreen frame into position were a flat profile of multi-section pieces at this time. The revised, single-piece A pillars from the easy-up hood were later modified, and also used with the traditional studded hood.

THE EASY-UP HOOD

This hood type was introduced in 2003, and was designed for those owners who prefer a simpler method of raising and lowering the hood. It has an inverted, U-shaped, chrome finish header rail, which

fits over the screen header frame with an over-centre catch at each end, and attaches to the inside of revised single-piece A pillars. There are two durable-dot fasteners on each side that fasten on to the hood frame, and one Tenax fastener each side that attaches to the B panel. For a while, some cars had durable-dot fasteners on to the B panel, but current cars have reverted to the Tenax fastener. At the rear, the easy-up hood is fixed to the body tub by two conical-headed, conventional-type bonnet fasteners, which are attached to the rear hood frame, with a cable-release handle in the driver's side interior B panel (on right-hand-drive cars).

The easy-up hood has a single plastic rear window panel, a more rounded profile, and slightly better headroom than the traditional studded hood. The hood remains visible when folded, and leaves the

A mohair easy-up hood photographed at the factory in June 2016. Note the single rear window, and that this type of hood frame sits on a rubber seal on the top edge of the rear panels. JOHN STRIDE

area behind the seats less exposed than the traditional studded hood (which removes completely). However, this hood type is almost as difficult to put up in a rainstorm as the traditional hood! It has the advantage of providing almost a tailgate access into the space behind the seats, as the rear can be lifted when the hood is in place by simply pulling the release lever inside the car. When doing this, the owner should first press down on the rear frame to relieve the pressure, and unfasten the Tenax fastener on each B panel, before lifting the rear of the hood. The rear section of the hood then rotates upwards around the frame pivot points, allowing access to the space behind the seats. Black is the most practical colour in either material.

Everflex is almost maintenance free, but may shrink in cold weather, and so in winter it should be left in the raised position. Mohair has a better, more luxurious look, but it may be more prone to damp patches on the seams, and so is likely to need more regular attention than Everflex. Mohair will also rub on itself when the hood lowered, and will create shiny patches and fold marks over time. Coloured Everflex or mohair can look very smart when new, but over time will discolour, and paler colours may prove difficult to clean satisfactorily. In the end this is down to personal choice. Everflex will resist most staining agents, but beware that mohair is easily marked by the environment so try to avoid parking under trees, where the sap may cause a green patchy fungal growth, and avoid bird droppings at all costs, especially near the coast.

Some hoods will leak, and the most common place for this to happen is over the windscreen header frame at speed. This problem can be minimized with careful application of neoprene channel. Sometimes a leak will suddenly appear at the top corner of the screen after parking up in heavy rain. It is strongly recommended to travel with a couple of towels, especially when on touring holidays. I will cover this in more detail in Chapters 3 and 12.

The hood lining may vary in colour. Generally, Everflex hoods will be black or grey inside, while mohair hoods will be black or creamy beige. Again, black is the most practical colour, but on a new build it will usually be whatever fabric is in stock at the time, as the interior lining colour doesn't feature as an option.

FOUR-SEATER MORGAN HOODS

Four-seaters have much larger and more complex hoods. The latest version of the four-seater hood is arguably the best looking, with rounded profile rear sidescreens; this hood usually shares the easy-up header rail. Unfortunately, the four-seater Morgan ceased production in November 2016. A variation of this body style might possibly be offered in the future as a two-seater Morgan with increased internal luggage space (or room for a dog).

So in summary, most people buy a Morgan to enjoy roof-down motoring, and the type of hood, and the colour, really shouldn't be a huge priority, especially when considering a used Morgan.

Storm Covers

It is recommended that owners carry a storm cover at all times, and use this to cover the cockpit, or the hood, whenever the Morgan is parked up. The storm cover is made of a water-resistant nylon type of material and is wipe clean. It will also keep the rain out when parked up in bad weather, and is a very worthwhile accessory. Storm covers are available from Morgan dealers and specialist suppliers, and will be covered in more detail in Chapter 12.

The Tonneau Cover

Before I begin this section, I must first clarify an important point: the tonneau is the open passenger compartment, while the tonneau cover covers this compartment!

The new options list includes a full tonneau cover and sidescreen bag to match the hood. These can be ordered for either style of hood. The tonneau cover will protect the whole cockpit area when fitted with the sidescreens removed. Where head restraints are fitted, these should be removed before fitting the tonneau cover, or alternatively the seats must be tilted or reclined. Some owners have had head restraint pockets fitted into their full tonneau cover, so that this is not necessary.

The standard full tonneau cover has a single centre zip, so when travelling alone, the passenger side can be covered. However, some owners find that the furled section of the tonneau cover on the driver's side interferes with seat-belt retraction, unless this section is folded very carefully. To get around this, some owners have invested in a three-zip tonneau cover: this style has two additional full-length zips, one on each side. This means that with the sidescreens removed, the two outer sides of the tonneau cover can remain fitted to the doors, and when the sections that cover the seats are furled, there is much less material involved, and it no longer interferes with seat-belt retraction.

Hood Cover

If the Morgan has no tonneau cover and has a traditional studded hood, when the hood is removed, the area behind the seats will be open to the elements. Also included in the new options list is a hood cover for the easy-up hood. The hood cover makes this hood look much tidier when lowered and still visible at the back of the car. These covers are made to match the hood material, and can be made up for a used Morgan on request, either by the factory, or by some dealers. For a while, leather hood covers were available from specialists, but these items are not currently advertised.

SEAT OPTIONS

There are four distinct types of seat available in the modern traditional Morgan. First there is the standard non-recliner, best identified by an inverted U shape in the backrest, with vertical flutes inside the

The non-reclining sports seats fitted to a Morgan with 'tombstone' head restraints. The distinctive inverted 'U' backrest pattern gives the game away.
DIRK MATTHEUS

Tilting and reclining sports seats in the trim and finishing area at the factory in April 2015. Note the contrasting piping, the second generation of head restraint, and the embroidery on the pair nearest the camera.

Performance seats photographed in almost the same place as the previous photograph, in October 2015. The head restraints are not yet fitted to the nearest pair. Note the horizontal stitching and side bolsters on the bases, and the shape of the head restraints. This batch was destined for the ARP4 (Aero Racing Plus 4).

U shape. This seat will only adjust fore and aft. These seats are not fitted into four-seaters because they would prevent access to the rear seats.

Second is the early version of the tilt/reclining seat, which can be identified by a well padded, but flat-contoured backrest, and was used in four-seaters. This type evolved into the third version, the sports (tilt/) recliner seat, which also has a tilt and recline function but with a bucket-contoured backrest. This makes it much easier to get the optimum backrest position, and the tilt function gives easier access into the space behind the seats, especially with the traditional studded hood. At the time of writing, the sports recliner has become the standard seat. Earlier two-seater Morgans had the non-recliner as standard, with the tilt/recliner as an option. Both seat versions have a similar base.

The more recent fourth and final seat option is the performance sports seat. This is easily identified by side bolsters in the seat base, and horizontal double-stitched panels, rather than the vertical stitched panels of the tilt/recliner. The performance seat also has a lumbar inflater in the backrest.

Most seats will be leather. Early base-model Morgan 4/4s had cloth seats, but these are exceptionally rare. Some cars may have rexine/vinyl seats but these are quite rare, and do look just like leather. There is a huge choice of colours and contrasting piping, so no two cars will be exactly the same. Contrasting stitching is available on the performance sports seats, and heated seats are available as an option on both. Perforated seat centre panels have been an option on the tilt/recliner, and waterproof leather is yet another option available at the time of writing.

HEAD RESTRAINTS

Head restraints in this period are all fixed with a single oval hole in the seat back, and an oval chromed fixing column. This design goes way back to 'British Leyland', and was common across the BL range in the 1970s. Initially the head restraints on the modern traditional Morgan were large and rectangular, and are sometimes referred to as 'tombstones'. The base of the head restraint touches the top of the seat backrest on the tilt/recliners, and the fixing column is therefore not visible when the head restraints are in their lowest position. These were the standard fit until 2006/7, when the design was slimmed down significantly, with an oval end profile.

The new style is very similar to the final style of head restraints used by BL in the 1980s. These restraints fit slightly proud of the seat backrest, and so now the chromed fixing column is visible by about 38mm (1.5in) in the lowest position. The performance sports seats have a redesigned, much more rounded head restraint, which is almost circular in end profile.

The Morgan logo may be embroidered on the head restraints as an extra cost option. In all cases the restraints are fitted well back, and some dealers will provide soft neck rolls that fit on to the head-restraint column to provide a bit more comfort, should you need it. If you buy a used Morgan without head restraints, you do have the option of sourcing head restraints at a reasonable price on-line from MG/Triumph suppliers.

Finally, take great care when adjusting any of these head restraints as they may be very stiff and uncooperative. If you need to remove them (when fitting the full tonneau cover, for example), you should pull up and rock the head restraint from side to side. Eventually it will suddenly come free, but take great care that it doesn't slip from your hands, because a flying head restraint can damage your Morgan bodywork.

BULKHEAD MATERIAL

The modern traditional Morgan comes with a stainless-steel bulkhead introduced in late 1997, and this should be hassle free. It is worth occasionally checking the tightness of the crosshead screws where the bulkhead joins the ash body frame, but that's really all there is to it. There will be a slight creep of the creamy grey sealing compound over time, because the relative movement as the chassis twists will squeeze the sealant out.

Should you sense a slight knock through the steering column, then check where the column passes through the bulkhead. Some cars have minimal clearance here, and may need the attention of a small file to build up some clearance. The steering column has two flats, which allow sufficient access for a file.

Earlier cars, before the 1997 changes, had a black-painted steel bulkhead. These will need more maintenance for obvious reasons, and you must keep a close eye on the lower edges, and deal with any paint defects and emerging corrosion. The limited edition ARP4 had a special aluminium bulkhead finished in red.

THE CHASSIS

Most Morgans have a chassis which is galvanized to inhibit corrosion. In early 2016 this treatment was discontinued and was replaced with an autophoretic coating, which is said to avoid the distortion caused by the hot galvanizing process. A handful of galvanized chassis were available into 2016 to special order. At the time of writing, the longevity of this new coating is therefore untested, but obviously I am keeping a close eye on it!

THE WHEELS

The standard Morgan 4/4 wheel is a 5 x 15in centrelock wire wheel; the standard Plus 4 wheel is a 6 x 15in centrelock wire wheel; and the standard Roadster wheel is a bolt-on alloy in the Plus 8 style, and these are 6.5 x 15in. The Plus 4 has the bolt-on alloy wheel as an extra cost option. Where centre-

Wire Wheel Specification

MWS (Motor Wheel Service) supply wire wheels to Morgan Motor Co., and have been involved in the manufacture and servicing of wire wheels for as long as I can remember. They are also a source of replacement wire wheels for a huge range of classic cars, and stock a wide range of accessories, including spinners. They can supply earless, two-eared or three-eared spinners, with or without the Morgan script, and some are available with an antique brass finish. They can also supply bolt-in tyre valves, which Morgan Motor Co. use on new builds. The MWS website is very informative and provides some useful technical information about Morgan wire wheels.

Inset, outset and back spacing: These terms refer to the alignment of the rim, relative to the wire wheel centre.

Inset is the distance by which the wheel rim centreline is inboard of the wheel centre inside edge.

Outset is the distance by which the wheel rim centreline is outboard of the wheel centre rear edge (I would call this the offset). Zero inset/outset means that the rear edge of the wheel centre is aligned with the rim centreline.

Back spacing is the distance between the wheel centre rear edge and the rim inner edge, and is quoted +/–3mm. The back spacing is critical on Morgans, because the inside edge of the tyre sidewall is extremely close to the crosshead, at the upper main spring mount. Interestingly, the 4/4 wheel has the most back spacing at 83mm, which only leaves a few millimetres clearance. When changing tyre size it is important to check the clearance at this point, and from personal experience I know that different brands of tyre in the same size do vary in sidewall width. Here is the data:

Morgan 4/4: Part number XW459. Size: 5 x 15in. Seventy-two spokes. Stainless steel, silver- or black-painted. Tyre size: 165R15. Inset/outset = 6.4mm inset; Back spacing = 83mm.

Morgan Plus 4: Part number XW5726. Size: 6 x15in. Seventy spokes. Stainless steel, silver- or black-painted. Tyre size: 195/60R15. Inset/outset = 10mm outset; Back spacing = 79.5mm.

Morgan Plus 8: Part number XW5719. Size: 7 x 16in. Sixty-six spokes. Stainless steel or chrome-plated. Tyre size: 205/55R16. Inset/outset = 27mm outset. Back spacing = 75mm.

Morgan LM62 Plus 8: Part number XW5765. Size: 6 x 16in. Sixty-six spokes. Stainless steel. Tyre size: 215/65R16. Inset/outset = 9mm outset. Back spacing = 81mm.

Morgan Roadster 2004 onwards, optional on later Roadster and Plus 4: Part number XW5777. Size: 7 x 16in. Seventy-two spokes. Stainless steel. Tyre size: 205/55R16. Inset/outset = 21mm outset. Back spacing = 80.5mm.

Morgan Roadster 2010 onwards: Black-painted standard fit from 2012. Part number XW5949. Size: 6.5 x 15in. Seventy-two spokes. Stainless steel or black-painted. Tyre size 195/60R15. Inset/outset = 15.6mm outset. Back spacing = 80mm.

lock wire wheels are ordered for a Roadster, they are 6.5 x 15in when ordered in black, or 7 x 16in when ordered in stainless steel. Centrelock alloys of 6.5 x 16in were an option on the Morgan Plus 8 for a short time (some sources quote these at 7in wide). Some limited-edition 4-cylinder cars had centrelock Minilite wheels (the Plus 4 Super Sport), or split rim Image alloy wheels on the Aero Racing Plus 4 (ARP4).

Some long-standing enthusiasts believe that all traditional Morgans really should have painted – or these days, powder-coated – wire wheels (although if you look back far enough, the standard fit was steel wheels with or without hubcaps). Four silver-finished wire wheels are the standard fit at the time of writing, with black or coloured wire wheels, and stainless-steel wire wheels as an extra cost option on the 4/4 and Plus 4. There is no doubt that silver-painted wires present a very traditional classic look, and hark back to the sports cars of the fifties and sixties. It is also true to say that wires finished in a colour to match the hood or upholstery present a very classic pre-war look.

All wire wheels take some serious time and effort to keep clean. Stainless steel is the easiest material to maintain because it is bare metal, and so can be polished back quite hard if it becomes dull or damaged. Paint or powder coating on any wire wheel will eventually be damaged by the spokes flexing and the balance weights, and paint chips will invite corrosion. When the tyres are replaced, inevitably there will be some damage to the paint or powder coating where the balance weights were attached. It may be possible to polish this out, but the wheels may need refinishing to restore their pristine look.

Current wire wheels are tubeless, and this is achieved by a black silicon band which is applied over the base of the spokes around the rim, when the wheels are manufactured. This coating may get damaged when the tyres are changed, either by careless use of a lever to remove the tyre, or due to the fragility of the silicon band when the inner edge of the tyre is pulled off the rim. The manufacturer, Motor Wheel Service (MWS), offers a refurbishment service if this happens.

To properly balance wire wheels, two special cones are required for the balancing machine, and the narrower rims don't have space for stick-on balance weights. Where traditional balance weights are fitted to the edge of the rim, note that some of these are steel, and may rust over time.

The recent Morgan 4/4 80th Anniversary has centrelock alloys designed to look like classic steel wheels, with circular holes around the centre, and some earlier 70th Anniversary cars had steel wheels with hubcaps, which are very appropriate for the period before wire wheels became common on sports cars. The weight and offset of each of these wheel types does affect the feel and handling of each Morgan. This is also influenced by the increasing weight of the engine in each model, because the engine weight and wheel size and offset increase together across the range.

THE SPARE WHEEL (OR NOT)

When the Morgan 4/4 Sport was introduced in 2008, it had no spare wheel. The spare wheel opening in the rear sloping panel was not cut out, and only a carefully crafted raised circle in the panel hinted at what, by rights, should have been there. Some owners love the look of this, but some do not! Leaving

A Morgan 4/4 on its 80th Anniversary with centrelock alloy wheels and no spare in May 2016. Note also the Morgan Motor Co. standard round door mirrors.

On the left is a Plus 4 four-seater with stainless wire wheels. This car has the standard door mirrors. On the right is a Plus 4 Super Sport. Note the bonnet scoop to the right, the lower valance, and the optional round door mirrors.

aside the issues of touring without a spare, I think that 'no spare' simply spoils the traditional shape, though many disagree. The Sport model ethos was extended to the Plus 4 and Roadster in 2010, and a small number of each has been produced. The Sport specification can still be ordered on new-builds, and the basic 'no cost' option at the time of writing is to have four road wheels and no spare.

TOOL KIT AND REAR STORAGE COMPARTMENT

Whereas bespoke Morgans have a tool tray under the rear decking inside the car, most Sport models do

not, although the tool kit (of a wheel-nut spanner and hammer) may still be present in a bag. Some Sport model cars have a carpeted compartment set into the rear panel, accessible from inside, which can take the sidescreens in their bag. It does appear though, that there are variations with Sport models as to what you get in terms of tool kit and rear storage compartment. A special luggage rack is available for Sport models, as is a spare-wheel carrier, which allows a spare wheel to be carried on the rack.

If you like the look of no spare wheel, but want the flexibility to carry one in the conventional cut-out in the rear panel, then the ARP4 provides the best of both worlds. This model has the conventional spare wheel set-up, but with an option of removing the spare and fitting a domed aluminium cover. Probably the biggest longer term issue with Sport models is the lack of easy access to the fuel tank, pump and charcoal canister, and the rear spring hangers. All are made much more accessible when the Morgan has a spare wheel opening in the rear panel.

BUMPERS OR OVER-RIDERS (OR NEITHER!)

There are three choices available on modern traditional Morgans: no bumpers and no over-riders is the first, 'no cost' option. Full bumpers front and rear is the second option. Over-riders front and rear is the third option. The brackets and fittings of bumpers or over-riders are different, so changing from one to the other on a used Morgan is an expensive option.

Some older Morgans have a full front bumper and over-riders at the rear (these fall outside the remit of this book). It may still be possible to order these on a new-build, if you seek a traditional 'period'-looking set-up. At the front, the appropriate mounting brackets are attached to the crosshead frame. In the case of over-riders, the track rods pass through the mounting brackets, and so these are fitted to the bare chassis early on in the build. At the front, the number-plate fixing is very different, depending on whether the choice is for full bumper or over-riders.

The current style of over-riders, with a front number-plate box, emerged with the Le Mans '62 Limited

A 4/4 with full bumpers, standard rectangular mirrors, and an easy-up hood. Note that the headlamp-to-cowl gap is small. The build number is 101419, and this Morgan is destined for dealer Allon White. STEVE HARRIS

A left-hand-drive 3.7-litre Roadster with over-riders and easy-up hood. Note the wide headlamp-to-cowl gap. This Morgan is also fitted with the optional wing top sidelamp units. Note the standard plastic interior mirror, and standard rectangular door mirrors. The build number is 101208. STEVE HARRIS

Edition cars in 2002. Here, the number-plate box was initially formed from aluminium, and included a short undertray; however, it soon became plastic/acrylic without an undertray, and the two recesses by which this box fixes to the front of the car have been enlarged since it was first introduced.

At the rear, the lower valance and number-plate mounting bracket are different for a full bumper than for over-riders. If there are to be no rear over-riders, the standard over-rider valance is fitted, but without the holes through which the brackets protrude. When over-riders are ordered, these two holes are cut into the rear valance before painting.

THE ENGINE CHOICES

Although at first sight the Morgan model range seems to consist of just three (four if we add the classic Plus 8), the choice is actually much wider

because of the engine and gearbox variations within each model.

Over the period under discussion, from 1997 the Morgan 4/4 has been available with two versions of the 1800cc Ford Zetec engine, the 1800cc Ford Duratec engine, and then the 1600cc Ford Sigma engine. The Morgan Plus 4 was available with the Rover 2-litre T16 engine and gearbox until the year 2000, and then it was not produced until 2004, when the model reappeared with the Ford 2-litre Duratec engine. Then in 2012 the Ford gearbox was changed to the Mazda gearbox on both models. There have also been special high performance editions of the Plus 4, the Plus 4 Super Sport, the Plus 4 Baby Doll (competition car) and the ARP4. All were produced in very limited numbers, with very limited bespoke options.

The classic Plus 8 (Rover V8) with a 3.9-litre or 4.6-litre engine was discontinued in 2004, and

A Roadster with over-riders and an easy-up hood. Note the optional round door mirrors. This Morgan was built for display at the Geneva Motor Show. STEVE HARRIS

immediately replaced with the 3-litre V6 Roadster, which has undergone three engine variations, each with slightly different power outputs, and two types of gearbox. The Series 1 was produced from 2004 to 2007, the Series 2 from 2007 to 2010, and the Series 3, with the wider front frame, from 2010 to 2012. The Roadster has also suffered from a wide range of 'road fund licence' costs, because its production has straddled some significant changes in taxation by emissions in the period between 2004 and 2008. There was a brief break in production of the Roadster in 2012 when Morgan Motor Co. were sourcing the 3.7-litre V6 engine with a six-speed gearbox from Ford in the USA.

Performance requirements are a very personal thing, so if you are not familiar with Morgan, you should try cars across the range before you commit to buy. You may be surprised to find that all Morgans have individual charms, and even outwardly identical cars of the same model may drive very differently. So if you seek to buy a Morgan, it is very important that you try a few cars so that you can understand this individuality.

Power steering: This became an option on the Plus 4 around 2013, and is standard on the 3.7-litre Roadster. It is electric, and speed sensitive. The motor attaches to the steering column, with a slight protrusion into the cockpit area. Power steering is also available as an aftermarket accessory from specialist suppliers.

Automatic transmission: This has also recently been developed by a specialist supplier for those potential owners who might prefer this transmission; however, it is a costly modification.

3-Litre V6 Roadster Ground Clearance

Ground clearance may be a crucial element in deciding which model will suit you best (for more detail, *see* Chapter 7). You might expect all traditional Morgans to be compromised on ground clearance, but all is not what it seems. The exhaust, which you might think would be vulnerable, is not. This is because from the manifold it emerges through the inner wing or valance panel, it is well secured under the wings, and is no lower than the chassis; in fact the only point where it may catch the road is at the tailpipe. This is low, and protrudes at the rear, which makes quite a shallow ramp angle, so when in a car park, or boarding or leaving a ferry, for example, the tailpipe may scrape the road.

The lowest point on most modern Morgans is the gearbox crossmember. This is an inverted U steel section, and it is vulnerable on some speed bumps. It is a strong section and will absorb most abuse, but some enthusiasts have strengthened it by fitting a flat steel skid plate under the inverted U. This will reduce clearance by the thickness of the steel, but being flat, it will be less likely to get stuck on a raised obstacle. This brings me to the 3-litre Roadster sump...

The Roadster sump is a very vulnerable cast aluminium component, and extreme care is necessary in avoiding speed bumps and centre posts for double gates. This sump has a sawtooth profile when viewed from the front (it was designed for a transverse application), and the lowest point is in line with the driver (on UK cars); this is also where the sump drain plug is situated. The lower edge of the sump sits below the level of the gearbox crossmember, and the thin aluminium casting can crack easily if impacted. This is a very important point, and needs to be considered when deciding which model is the right one for you.

A 3-litre V6 Roadster sump, photographed from the front. The gearbox crossmember is just visible behind the sump. The vulnerable angled bottom edge is clear.

The offside view of the sump, showing the level of exposure. The gearbox crossmember is to the left.

IN CONCLUSION

If you are seeking to buy your first Morgan, then do your research thoroughly and take your time. Make an effort to visit the Morgan factory, and take a guided tour. Seriously consider joining the Morgan Sports Car Club before you buy, and contact your local group; they will be delighted to share their knowledge and experiences.

Visit a number of Morgan dealers, and find one that is on your wavelength: you will be made very welcome. It doesn't have to be the dealer nearest to where you live. Rule nothing out, and try as many Morgans as you can, in order to understand which model suits you best. Join *Talk Morgan*, which will provide a hugely valuable source of information and advice, especially for a potential first time buyer.

It is sometimes said that it can take up to two years to sort out a new Morgan, and this is why some enthusiasts prefer to buy a used car, which has done some miles, and had the bugs ironed out. My experience of buying my Roadster at three years old is that it has proved to be well sorted and a delight to own. Similarly, our 4/4 Anniversary which had done 19,300km (12,000 miles) in the first year was also a well sorted car. I knew that buying a new Plus 4 might provide some challenges, but a year in, it has been fine. Having done 4,000km (2,500 miles) at the time of writing it is loosening up nicely and is a pleasure to drive.

TECHNICAL SPECIFICATIONS

This section gives the technical specifications for each standard model, in the period from 1997 to 2017. In addition to the three models in production at the time of writing there have been earlier versions of each model, each with engine and gearbox variations. My starting point for collecting and collating this information has been the Morgan Motor Co. owner's handbooks, and the website of Morgan Motor Co. I have also used the official sales brochures that cover this period (1997 to 2017). Not all the available information can be considered as being completely accurate, so I have also searched on-line, and collected and compared a large amount of relevant data.

In addition I have taken measurements from specific Morgans in order to validate the true dimensions, which are often confusing, even from reliable sources. In respect of the overall vehicle dimensions, the front and rear track is quoted for wire wheels. Where bolt-on alloys are optional, these will alter the track dimensions very slightly, but the changes front and

rear will also differ slightly due to the way the wheels fit on to the hubs. The wheelbase was lengthened by 2cm (0.75in) in 2006, and this is reflected in the specifications. The crosshead was widened by 8.25cm (3.25in) in 2010, and this has also been reflected in the data.

When measuring the overall width of a Morgan, the widest point, excluding door mirrors, will be across the rear wings, except for the 4/4. This is because the centrelock spinners on the 4/4 wheels protrude beyond the wings, and so the overall width of the 4/4 is closer than you might imagine to the width of the Plus 4. The overall length of each Morgan will vary according to whether full bumpers are fitted or not. If no bumpers or over-riders are fitted, the overall length will be less. Some luggage racks overhang the rear, and so will add to the overall length. All of this is relevant if your garage length is critical.

The published dry weights must always be regarded as a guide, and may be conservative. Generally speaking, the engine data is well documented, and can be cross-checked across a number of sources on-line. The gearbox data is less well documented, and this becomes quite difficult to establish when a number of ratios were available, for example with the Ford MT-75 unit.

All quoted dates and years of change must be regarded as a guide only, and all data provided is to the best of my knowledge, and is as accurate as I can make it at the time of writing.

I have not included engine data for the three limited-edition, performance-based Plus 4 Models in the technical specifications. These were the Plus 4 Super Sport with a variable cam engine and 200bhp, the Baby Doll with a 250bhp Omex engine, and the Aero Racing Plus 4, which has 2-litre Cosworth Power and 225bhp. These cars were built in such limited numbers that they rarely come up for sale, and details of the engine specification of each model is very difficult to track down. Similarly, the Aero Racing V6 Roadster, which is a pure competition Morgan, is outside the scope of this book.

With regard to the front suspension, the Morgan stub axles slide on a fixed pin (kingpin), so I use the term 'sliding stub axles' (for more detail, see Chapter 8).

Morgan 4/4 (1997 to 2008); Morgan 4/4 (from 2008)

The current production model specification is quoted first. Where specification is different, 1997 to 2000 is noted with a single star asterisk*.

Note that the Ford Zetec Silver Top was introduced in 1993 in short-door cars. Up until 1999 these were built with a Gemmer steering box. A steering rack (Jack Knight) was optional. From 1999 to 2001, the 4/4 was built with rack and pinion, with a quick steering-rack option (three turns lock to lock).

The Ford Zetec Black Top was used from 2001 to 2005, and was replaced with the Ford Duratec from 2005 to 2008. The 4/4 was fitted with a Quaife steering rack of 3.5 turns lock to lock from around 2005.

Layout and chassis
Autophoretic-coated steel chassis. Galvanized up to 2016. Ash-framed body. Stainless-steel bulkhead. Aluminium body

Engine

Type**	Ford Sigma: 1595cc from 2008 *to 2005 Ford Zetec: 1796cc; to 2008 Ford Duratec: 1798cc
Block material	Aluminium *to 2005 Ford Zetec: cast iron
Head material	Aluminium
Cylinders	In-line four
Cooling	Water
Bore and stroke	79 x 81.4mm *Zetec: 80.6 x 88mm; Duratec: 83.0 x 83.1mm
Capacity	1595cc *Zetec: 1796cc; Duratec: 1798cc
Valves	16v dohc
Compression ratio	10:1 *Zetec 10:1; Duratec: 10.8:1
Carburettor	Fuel injection
Max. power	110bhp @ 6,000rpm *Zetec: 111bhp @ 5,800rpm; Duratec: 125bhp @ 6,100rpm
Max. torque	131Nm (97lb/ft) @ 5,750rpm *Zetec 150Nm (110lb/ft) @ 4,500rpm; Duratec: 162Nm (119lb/ft) @ 4,600rpm
Fuel capacity	55ltr (12 imp. gallons) *50ltr (11 imp. gallons)

Transmission

Gearbox	To 2012: Ford MT-75 five-speed. From 2012: Mazda MX5 five-speed
Clutch	Hydraulically operated diaphragm clutch
Ratios	1st: Ford: 3.87:1. Mazda: 3.14:1. *Zetec 3.89:1
	2nd: Ford: 2.08:1. Mazda: 1.89:1
	3rd: Ford: 1.36:1. Mazda: 1.33:1. *Zetec 1.34:1
	4th: Ford and Mazda: 1:1
	5th: Ford: 0.76:1. Mazda: 0.81:1. *Zetec 0.82:1
Reverse:	Ford: 3.49:1. Mazda: 3.58:1. *Zetec 3.51:1. *Duratec 3.26:1
Final drive	3.73:1; optional 4:1:1. *Zetec 4.1:1

Suspension and steering

Front	Independent by sliding stub axle and coil springs. Telescopic dampers
Rear	Live axle with leaf springs. Telescopic dampers
Steering	Rack and pinion *Steering box 1997 to 1999, rack optional
Tyres	165/80 x 15in radial
Wheels	Wire spoke wheels. Optional centrelock alloys on 80th Anniversary *Standard bolt-on steel wheels on 70th Anniversary
Rim width	5in x 15in

Brakes

Type	Front discs, rear drums. Twin circuit with servo.
Size	11in discs. 9in drums

Dimensions

Track (wire wheels)	
Front	1,238mm (48.75in) *1,222mm (48in)
Rear	1,400mm (55.25in) *1,384mm (55in)
Wheelbase	2,502mm (98.5in) *2,483mm (97.75in)
Overall length	3,890mm (153in) with over-riders; 4,010mm (157.9in) with full bumpers
Overall width	1,645mm (64.75in). Protruding centrelock nuts are the widest point
Overall height	1,220mm (48in)
Unladen weight	800kg (1,764lb) *820kg (1,808lb)

Performance

Top speed	115mph (185km/h)
0–62mph	8.0sec

Morgan Plus 4 (1997 to 2000): Morgan Plus 4 (from 2004 to 2013. Not produced between 2000 and 2004); Morgan Plus 4 (from 2013)

The current production model specification is quoted first. Where specification is different, 1997 to 2000 is noted with a single star asterisk *, 2004 to 2013 is noted with a two star asterisk **.

Layout and chassis
Autophoretic-coated steel chassis. Galvanized up to 2016. Ash-framed body. Stainless-steel bulkhead. Aluminium body.

Engine

Type	Ford GDI 1999cc
	*Rover T16 2000cc
	**Ford Duratec 2000cc
Block material	Aluminium *Cast iron
Head material	Aluminium
Cylinders	In-line four
Cooling	Water
Bore and stroke	87.5 x 83.1mm
	*84.5 x 89mm
Capacity	1999cc *1994cc
Valves	16v dohc
Compression ratio	12:1 *10:1 **10:1
Carburettor	GDI (gasoline direct injection)
	*Fuel injection **Fuel injection
Max. power	154bhp @ 6,000rpm
	*136bhp @ 6,000rpm
	**145bhp @ 6,100rpm
Max. torque	201Nm (148lb/ft) @ 4,450rpm
	*187Nm (138lb/ft) @ 2,500rpm
	**187Nm (138lb/ft) @ 4,500rpm
Fuel capacity	55ltr (12 imp. gallons)

Transmission

Gearbox	Mazda MX5 five-speed
	*Rover R380 five-speed
	**Ford MT-75 five-speed
	(from 2012, Mazda MX5 five-speed)
Clutch	Hydraulically operated diaphragm clutch
Ratios	1st: 3.14:1
	*3.32:1
	**3.87:1
	2nd: 1.89:1
	*2.087:1
	**2.08:1
	3rd: 1.33:1
	*1.397:1 **1.36:1
	4th: 1:1
	5th: 0.81:1
	*0.79:1
	**0.76:1
	Reverse: 3.58:1
	*3.43:1
	**3.49:1
Final drive	3.73:1

Suspension and steering

Front	Independent by sliding stub axle and coil springs. Telescopic dampers
Rear	Live axle with leaf springs. Telescopic dampers
Steering	Rack and pinion. Optional electric power steering
Tyres	195/60 x 15in
Wheels	Wire spoke wheels. Optional bolt-on alloys
Rim width	6 x 15in wire spoke. 6.5 x 15in bolt-on alloys

Brakes

Type	Front discs, rear drums. Twin circuit with servo
Size	11in discs. 9in drums

Dimensions

Track (wire wheels)	
Front	1,350mm (53.2in)
	*1,290mm (50.8in)
	**1,275mm (50.2in) to 2010
Rear	1,454mm (57.25in)
	*1,440mm (56.7in)
Wheelbase	2,502mm (98.5in)
	*/**2,483mm (97.75in) to 2006
Overall length	3,890mm (153in) with over-riders; 4,010mm (157.9in) with full bumpers
Overall width	1,651mm (65in)
	*/**1,626mm (64in)
Overall height	1,220mm (48in)
Unladen weight	927kg (2,044lb)
	*800kg (1,764lb)
	**900kg (1,984lb)

Performance

Top speed	118mph (190km/h)
	*118mph (190km/h)
	**120mph (193km/h)
0–62mph	7.5sec
	*/**7.3 sec

Morgan Plus 8 (1997 to 2004)

Layout and chassis
Galvanized steel chassis. Ash-framed body.
Stainless-steel bulkhead. Aluminium body.

Engine

Type	Rover V8 3900cc or 4600cc
Block material	Aluminium
Head material	Aluminium
Cylinders	90-degree V8
Cooling	Water
Bore and stroke	94 x 71.2mm; 94 x 82mm
Capacity	3946cc; 4555cc
Valves	16v single cam, pushrods
Compression ratio	9.35:1
Carburettor	Fuel injection
Max. power	190bhp @ 4,800rpm; 194.4bhp @ 4,400rpm
Max. torque	305Nm (225lb/ft) @ 3,500rpm; 352Nm (260lb/ft) @ 3,000rpm
Fuel capacity	55ltr (12 imp. gallons)

Transmission

Gearbox	Rover R380 five-speed
Clutch	Hydraulically operated diaphragm clutch
Ratios	1st: 3.32:1
	2nd: 2.087:1
	3rd: 1.397:1
	4th: 1:1
	5th: 0.79:1
	Reverse: 3.43:1
Final drive	3.08:1

Suspension and steering

Front	Independent by sliding stub axle and coil springs. Telescopic dampers
Rear	Live axle with leaf springs. Telescopic dampers
Steering	Rack and pinion
Tyres	205/55 x 16in or 205/60 x 15in
Wheels	Bolt-on alloys. Optional wire spoke wheels. Optional centre-lock alloys for a limited period
Rim width	6.5 x 15in bolt-on alloys; 7 x 16in wire spoke; 7 x16in centrelock alloys

Brakes

Type	Front discs, rear drums. Twin circuit with servo
Size	11in discs. 9in drums

Dimensions

Track (wire wheels)	
Front	1,300mm (51.25in)
Rear	1,480mm (58.25in)
Wheelbase	2,483mm (97.75in)
Overall length	3,890mm (153in) with over-riders; 4,010mm (157.9in) with full bumpers
Overall width	1,680mm (66in)
Overall height	1,220mm (48in)
Unladen weight	940kg (2,072lb)

Performance

Top speed	124mph (200km/h)
0–62mph	6.7sec

Morgan 3.0-litre V6 Roadster: Series 1: 2004 to 2007; Series 2: 2007 to 2010; Series 3: 2010 to 2012; Morgan 3.7-litre V6 Roadster (from 2012)

The current production model specification is quoted first. Where specification is different for the earlier series, it is noted with a single star asterisk *.

Layout and chassis
Autophoretic-coated steel chassis. Galvanized up to 2016. Ash-framed body. Stainless-steel bulkhead. Aluminium body

Engine

Type	Ford 3.7-litre Cyclone V6.
	*S1/S2/S3: Ford 3.0-litre Duratec V6
Block material	Aluminium
Head material	Aluminium
Cylinders	60-degree V6
Cooling	Water
Bore and stroke	95.5 x 86.7mm;
	*89 x 79.5mm
Capacity	3726cc;
	*2967cc
Valves	24v dohc
Compression ratio	10:1
Carburettor	Fuel injection
Max. power	280bhp @ 6,000rpm
	*S1: 223bhp @ 6,150rpm; S2: 201bhp @ 6,100rpm; S3: 240bhp @ 6,550rpm
Max. torque	379.6Nm (280lb/ft) @ 4,500rpm
	*S1: 279Nm (206lb/ft) @ 4,900rpm; S2: 264Nm (194lb/ft) @ 4,500rpm; S3: 302Nm (223lb/ft) @ 4,300rpm
Fuel capacity	55ltr (12 imp. gallons)

Transmission

Gearbox	Ford/Getrag MT-82 six-speed
	*S1: Getrag 221 five-speed; S2 and S3: Ford MT-75 five-speed
Clutch	Hydraulically operated diaphragm clutch
Ratios	1st: 4.236:1
	*S1: 4.23:1; S2 and S3: 3.87:1
	2nd: 2.538:1
	*S1: 2.52:1; S2 and S3: 2.08:1
	3rd: 1.665:1
	*S1: 1.67:1; S2 and S3: 1.36:1
	4th: 1.2387:1
	*S1: 1.22:1; S2 and S3: 1:1
	5th: 1:1
	*S1: 1:1; S2 and S3: 0.76:1
	6th: 0.704:1

	Reverse: 3.32:1
	*S1: 3.51:1 S2 and S3: 3.49:1
Final drive	3.08:1
	*S1: 3.08:1 S2 and S3: 3.73:1

Suspension and steering

Front	Independent by sliding stub axle and coil springs. Telescopic dampers
Rear	Live axle with leaf springs. Telescopic dampers. Anti-tramp bars
	*S1 and S2 no anti-tramp bars; S3 single anti-tramp bar
Steering	Rack and pinion. Electric power steering
Tyres	205/55 x 16in or 205/60 x 15in
Wheels	Wire spoke wheels. Optional bolt-on alloys
Rim width	6.5 x 15in black wire spoke. 7 x 16in stainless wire spoke. 6.5 x 15in bolt-on alloys

Brakes

Type	Front discs, rear drums. Twin circuit with servo
Size	11in discs. 9in drums

Dimensions

Track (wire wheels)	
Front	1,375mm (54.2in)
	*S1 and S2: 1,300mm (51.25in); S3: 1,375mm (54.2in)
Rear	1,480mm (58.25in)
Wheelbase	2,502mm (98.5in)
	*S1 to 2006: 2,483mm (97.75in)
Overall length	3,890mm (153in) with over-riders; 4,010mm (157.9in) with full bumpers
Overall width	1,680mm (66in)
Overall height	1,220mm (48in)
Unladen weight	950kg (2,094lb)
	*S1, S2, S3: 940kg (2,072lb)

Performance

Top speed	140mph (225km/h)
	*S1, S2, S3: 134mph (216km/h)
0–62mph	5.5sec
	*S1: 5.0sec

CHAPTER TWO

MAKING YOURSELF COMFORTABLE

A traditional Morgan is surprisingly comfortable, which might come as a surprise to some. After reading many road test reviews over the years, I had built up certain expectations; however, on my first test drive in 2008, these expectations were quickly dashed! But there are ways of making things even more comfortable in the cockpit.

DASHBOARD DESIGN

The dashboard options available when ordering a new Morgan are to have either a painted finish, a leather-covered dashboard, or one finished in a walnut veneer. If you are fortunate enough to be able to make a Morgan Motor Co. factory visit, you will witness the superb quality that can be achieved by expert craftsmen with veneers, using their vacuum press and layers of lacquer. More recently, alternative wood finishes have been made available on new-builds, in ash, brown velvet, burbinga and zebrano – but walnut remains a popular choice on traditional cars. Samples of the other veneers are rather thin on the ground, and so in 2016 we opted for walnut as a safe choice for our Plus 4.

Depending on the build year of a Morgan and the chosen finish, some dashboards will have a glovebox lid, and some will have an open glovebox. Where there is an open-fronted glovebox, black elasticated cargo netting may be fitted to retain the contents – but not all the open fronts have netting. Earlier

The dashboard used from 2003 to 2007. The switches are brightly coloured and control the heater fan, the rear foglamp, the heated screen and the hazard lights. Above these four switches are ten warning lights in a single row. The glovebox is bottom hinged with a push-button lockable catch.

glovebox lids were bottom hinged with a protruding push-button, lockable catch towards the top. At the time of writing, the current glovebox lids are top hinged with a press-to-open, press-to-close arrangement, without a lock.

You will spend many hours looking at your dashboard, so it's very important to get the style right! My preferred dashboard layout was quite short lived, being adopted in late 2003. This is a six-gauge design, with the revcounter and speedometer in front of the driver, and four small gauges almost across the centreline of the dashboard, but offset by one gauge away from the driver: these are a voltmeter, oil pressure gauge, water temperature gauge and fuel gauge. The background is ivory with black numerals.

This ivory gauge dashboard replaced the earlier similar design, which had gauges with black backgrounds, but with the four small supplementary gauges in a 'two-over-two' arrangement in the centre of the dash. The 2003 replacement dashboard is quite shallow, and recessed under the bulkhead panel. The mileometer (odometer) and tripmeter on the 2003 version is small, and can be difficult to read without having the sidelights on.

At some point during 2007 the dashboard design reverted to the more traditional Morgan layout, with black backgrounds and with two large gauges across the centre of the dash, recessed into an inverted isosceles trapezoid panel, with rounded corners. These were the speedometer and a three-function unit containing fuel gauge, oil pressure gauge and water temperature gauge. On this dashboard, the revcounter is a separate unit, and is mounted in front of the driver. Some Morgans have this gauge centred exactly on the steering column, but on some cars it is slightly offset. With either dashboard design, a matching clock was an optional extra, and when selected from the options list, was mounted to the right of the steering wheel on right-hand-drive cars.

Which of these options you might prefer is very much a personal choice. Underneath the post-2003 dashboard there is no closing trim panel, and so the underdash area is exposed to the elements (the cold and damp). This can benefit from having a DIY trim panel fitted, but the revised dashboard from 2007 comes with a shaped black plastic trim panel across the width of the underside of the dashboard, which is secured with small screws into the bottom edge of the dashboard.

A painted Morgan 4/4 dashboard in 'Porsche Bahama Yellow' with open glovebox and cargo net, at the factory. This was destined to be one of the Geneva show cars in 2017. JOHN STRIDE

A Plus 4 Super Sport in build at the factory, with a light ash dashboard and Brooklands steering wheel.

There is one other important difference between the two dashboard types. Since the earlier (ivory background) dash is shallower than the 2007 replacement, this allows greater upward movement of the adjustable steering column. This means that there is more space between the bottom of the steering wheel and the driver's seat base. The reality of either dashboard is that most owners need the steering column to be set at the highest point for ease of access.

As with all things Morgan, these change points can be rather indistinct. Because there is no conventional production line, at the point of change cars will pass through the factory with either specification. In addition, owners can specify some non-standard items at extra cost, and aftermarket dashboards are readily available, and so the dashboard in particular is not a firm indicator of exactly when any Morgan was built. The Plus 4 Super Sport limited edition of 2011/12 came with a light ash dashboard in the style of the 2007 item.

When the 3.7-litre V6 Roadster was introduced in 2013, it came with a new bespoke dashboard specific to that engine type, with two extra-large gauges mounted centrally, and the fuel gauge and water temperature gauge fitted in between. These two large

gauges have a 180-degree sweep inside standard but large circular bezels. The two smaller gauges have a less than 180-degree sweep in a surround that is hard to describe but is rather loaf shaped. The clock is in front of the driver, recessed into a contrasting panel.

When the Plus 4 GDI was introduced in 2014, it came with a simplified dashboard, where the speedometer and revcounter were mounted centrally, and the water temperature and fuel gauges were mounted in front of the driver. There is no oil pressure gauge on the Plus 4 GDI, which some traditionalists regret, but a clock is mounted centrally between the main gauges as a standard fit. These instruments are brightly lit with quite attractive yellow detailing. An instrument panel light dimmer switch is included, and is normally fitted under the dash, on the right on right-hand-drive cars.

The limited edition ARP4 was provided with a modified version of this dashboard with ivory-backed instruments, in a style similar to the contemporary Aero 8 instruments. Meanwhile, the 4/4 model has continued with the traditional 'post-2007' dashboard, with two main centre gauges and the revcounter in front of the driver. As vehicle electronics progress, it seems that bespoke instruments that are dictated by the engine electronics are becoming, and will become, the norm.

A walnut Plus 4 GDI dashboard on the assembly bench at the factory.

A Plus 4 GDI dashboard fitted into the car. Note the build book ahead of the gearstick.
JOHN STRIDE

A 3.7-litre V6 Roadster, with a painted dashboard and an open glovebox with cargo net. The order number appears to be 101159. The blue tape on the right-hand-side dashboard top notes 'side lights'. JOHN STRIDE

ADJUSTING THE SEATS

Morgans fitted with the shallower (post-2003 ivory background) dashboard were fitted with tapered wooden spacers under the seat runners. These spacers tapered from front to rear. When the deeper dashboard was introduced, it impacted on the distance between the seat base and the bottom of the steering wheel, and from that point in time it appears there were no seat spacers fitted and the seats were bolted straight on to the carpet and floorboards. These seat runners each have one protruding bolt tail with a nut attached, and without the wooden spacers, this nut presses into the floor and can make the seat adjustment rather stiff, because it distorts the seat runners. However, the benefit of having no spacers is that there is more room under the steering wheel, and this makes it much easier to get in and out. This flexibility does mean that it is very easy to set up the seat height and the tilt of the base to your personal preference.

Each seat is secured by six bolts and nuts, which pass through the chassis and floor boards. The rear pair of fasteners on each seat pass through the main double-skinned crossmember ahead of the rear wheels, and so are slightly longer than the other four fasteners. It doesn't take long to lift a seat by removing the six fasteners, and this can easily be done single-handed. But note that if there is a seat-belt sensor in the driver's seat, it must first be unplugged, and this small plug may be fiddly to release. The seat can be folded forwards (remove the head restraint first), and rested upturned on the rear shelf. This is a much safer option than lifting the seat out over the rear wing!

Once the seat is out of the way, spacers of wood, or metal washers, may be added or removed under the runners until the height and rake of the seat base are exactly right for the owner. This is a job I have always undertaken in a variety of cars over the years when there was no height or seat base adjustment, and although it takes a while to get this just right, it then stays right, and comfortable, for good. The correct length bolts will be needed if the seat height is raised. No more than one inch should be necessary, because more than this may make getting in and out difficult.

CLEANING THE CARPETS AND FLOORBOARDS

Taking the seats out also presents the perfect opportunity to clean the carpets, and to clean and treat the floorboards. An amazing amount of sawdust and debris seems to collect under the seats. Danish Oil is one option for applying to the floorboards, as it is quick drying, but other wood preservative and waterproofing products are available. The leather inner sill trim is stapled to the floorboards, and to remove this trim to inspect the floorboards underneath is very time-consuming as each staple has to be carefully removed. Some owners do this, and then devise a simpler method of holding down the leather trim; durable dot fasteners would be one way of doing this.

The padding under the inner sill panels can become wet over time, and so invariably at some point the leather trim will need lifting for inspection. Otherwise, if wet for a long period, the timber frame may begin to rot under the doors. Replacement fibreglass panels are available, which can be fitted under the inner sill leather trim, replacing the standard padding. Closed-cell neoprene could also be used as replacement padding.

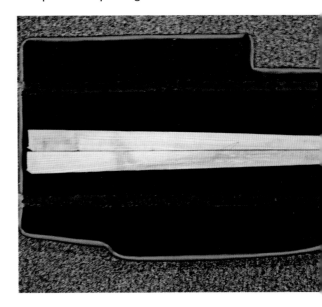

The tapered seat-runner spacers from a 2005 Morgan. The carpet is offside, and front is to the left in the image. The holes in the carpet are just visible.

The tapered seat-runner spacers were unpainted as standard. They are at crossmember height at the front, and half that height at the rear. Later cars with the deeper dashboard don't have wooden spacers. Note the stainless-steel chassis-rail cover plate, a popular accessory.

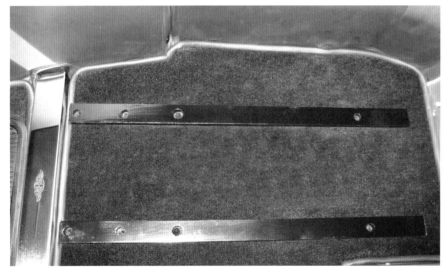

These spacers are 12mm (½in) thick and home-made, to lift the seat slightly. The third holes along from the left are to accommodate the nut that protrudes from the seat runners. Note the chassis-rail stainless cover plate on the left.

The performance sports seats have an inflatable lumbar support, and these are also available as aftermarket accessories. An alternative solution is 4mm standard density neoprene sheet, doubled over and glued together. This can be slid behind the backrest and will provide additional support.

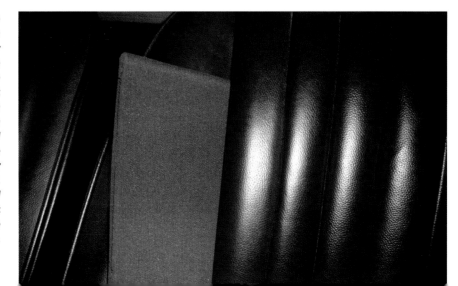

Carpet or Rubber Mats

Some owners will fit an additional rubber mat, or carpet square over the floor carpets to prevent wear. A variety of carpet mats or rubber mats are available for the owner who wishes to do this.

COCKPIT REPLACEMENTS AND MODIFICATIONS

THE STEERING WHEEL

The very first item usually replaced on a new Morgan is the standard steering wheel. This is a generic wheel, designed to pass the new build regulations, but it is not attractive! 'Moto-Lita' is the current steering wheel of choice for the enthusiast, but other brands are available. They come in a variety of diameters, flat or dished, and with a leather or wooden rim. This is a very personal choice, and my preference is the flat 14in Moto-Lita, with a black leather rim. I don't really get on with woodrim steering wheels, as I find them too hard and slippery in hot weather, but a thicker woodrim is also now available, which is more comfortable than the earlier thin woodrim steering wheels.

If you find the gap between the steering wheel and seat base is tight, making it difficult to get in and out, there is a further option of an offset steering wheel, where the wheel centre is drilled below the centre point. This means that the steering wheel is located higher when straight ahead, but when turned will follow an eccentric path. More recently there are options of flat-bottomed or removable steering wheels.

There are also several different boss designs, which affect both the look as the boss enters the column shroud, and the position of the steering wheel relative to the driver. The choice is wide ranging. Some bosses create a rather distracting reflection in the windscreen, so beware of very shiny bosses! With a flat or dished steering wheel and the right boss design, you should be able to get the steering wheel rim in just the right place to suit your stature.

REAR-VIEW MIRROR

The second most popular modification is to replace the large plastic rear-view mirror with a smaller, more classic unit. More recently this option has been available direct from the factory as an optional extra. The replacement classic mirror may be smaller than the standard item, but visually is a huge improvement. These mirrors are also available from dealers and specialists in two sizes, and also as a dash top mount, and a rod mount. You should talk to your dealer about suitability because the latter two options may not be suitable for certain Morgans.

Note that on hot summer days, when parked with the roof down and with the sun behind the car, on very rare occasions the sun's rays can sometimes reflect from the rear-view mirror and focus on the head restraints. As the sun moves across the sky, it may then burn a line in the head restraint, and this damage may be mistaken for vandalism. Therefore when parked in the hot sun, either adjust the rear-view mirror downwards, or hang a duster or hat over it!

CHASSIS CROSSMEMBERS

The chassis crossmembers are exposed and visible in front of the seats, and a popular modification is to add stainless-steel cover plates. These were originally designed by, and available only from, John Worrall of Heart of England Morgans. The stainless-steel covers are available with an etched logo, and simply slot over the crossmembers, after easing the leather transmission tunnel cover out of the way. These covers are now more widely available, and if you decide to order these items, you must specify the year and model. Certain models, such as the 3.7-litre Roadster, need slightly shorter covers due to the extra transmission tunnel width.

AFTERMARKET DASHBOARDS

Aftermarket dashboards are available from a small number of specialist suppliers, and you may enhance your existing dashboard by adding a clock, stainless instrument bezels, retro-styled indicator stalks, or a leather-trimmed steering-column cowl. All these accessories are available if you search on-line, consult your dealer, or ask the experts at your local MSCC group. More upgrades are available in the form of chrome/stainless door-lock covers, and a centre

The prototype ARP4, on the Morgan Motor Co. stand at the Silverstone Classic in July 2015. Note the brushed aluminium door trims and attractive dashboard, only available on this limited edition model. Note also the performance sports seats with embroidered head restraints and unique chassis-rail covers, which expose the red chassis.

armrest with or without a trinket tray, in a leather finish to match your upholstery.

DOOR MIRRORS

A very popular exterior improvement is to replace the original door mirrors with aftermarket stainless mirror heads, or complete mirrors and bases. Two versions of door mirrors are fitted by the factory: oblong mirrors are the standard fit, but the offside (passenger side) provides a very limited field of vision. A pair of round mirrors are available as a new option, and these are rather better. However, aftermarket mirrors, some of which are available with convex glass, make a huge improvement to rear vision on both sides, and being stainless steel, will last much longer and resist tarnishing. (For more on general accessories, see Chapter 6.)

SIDESCREEN LINERS

Some owners opt for leather sidescreen trim/liners, which fit between the side window channel and the top of the door. These trim panels cover the almost vertical sidescreen mounting bars, which secure the sidescreens to the doors. With an Everflex hood come Everflex sidescreen panels, and these can be improved by adding a panel of mohair to the inside of

The Edges of the Doors

The trailing edge of each door is painted ash, and it is not a difficult job to improve this look by adding a leather trim panel down the edge of each door. The secret in getting a good finish is to source thin and supple leather. My preference for black upholstery makes this much simpler, although leather can be dyed, and kits are available on-line. Using a thick brown paper template as a pattern, the leather can be trimmed to shape with sharp scissors, and stuck on to double-sided tape with the edges turned over. The double-sided tape then secures the trim panel to the edge of the door, from the padded rail along the top edge, down as far as the curved corner, but not along the door bottom (see photograph). Once the shape has been finalized, this becomes a simple and worthwhile improvement.

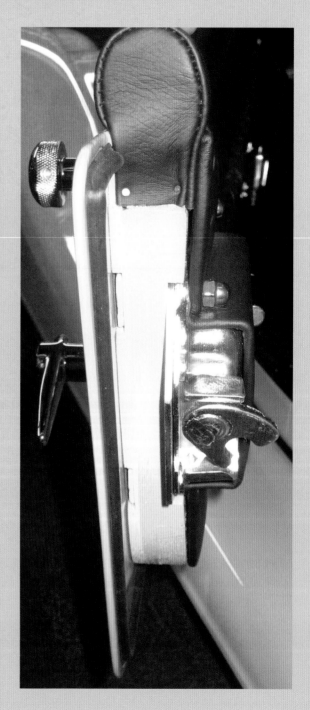

RIGHT: *The edge of the door from the factory is painted ash...*

FAR RIGHT:*...and this is the result, after a fine leather offcut is shaped round a template of double-sided tape and attached to the door. The lower edge of the leather is just out of sight under the door.*

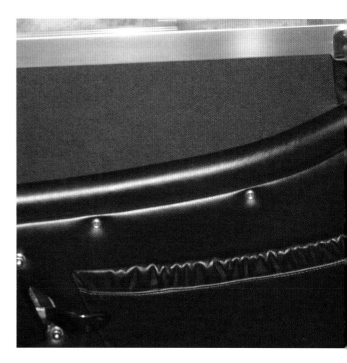

The leather trim added to the sidescreen frame. It's a simple matter to remove the lower panel and add the trim using double-sided tape, then tuck it behind the frame. Don't overtighten the screws, and use Locktite.

the panel using aerosol adhesive. In addition, the bare aluminium sidescreen mounting bars may be trimmed with leather, secured with double-sided tape. Leather offcuts can be sourced from the internet.

THE THROTTLE PEDAL

Before moving on from the cockpit area, there is one more quite important thing to mention. Morgans fitted with a conventional accelerator cable come with a roller throttle pedal as standard. This quirky feature is very much an acquired taste, and some owners swear by it, but others don't get on with it at all. The good news is that an organ throttle pedal can be easily fitted over the roller, which transforms the feel. The organ pedal was an option on the new price list and can be retro fitted to all cars with the roller pedal. Note that early rollers are metal and later rollers are plastic, and you will need to order a compatible organ pedal. Some organ pedals come with a hoop casting at the rear which takes the roller,

The roller accelerator pedal, which comes as standard. There are no pedal rubbers on this Morgan, which can be an MOT fail in certain territories, and there is no carpet fitted to the bulkhead. ROGER GATES

The roller behind the narrow section of this organ accelerator pedal; it locates inside a metal casting. Note also the pedal rubbers, which are not expensive but don't seem to last long. Some owners use skateboard grip tape on the pedals instead of rubbers.

A 2016 Plus 4 GDI drive by wire throttle. The mechanical brake-light switch is also visible between the inclined black rectangle and the horizontal metal plate.

but some are a simple flat piece of metal, which rests on the roller.

As you will be aware, engineering detail evolves, and with the 4/4 Sport in 2008, the 3.7 Roadster in 2013, and the Plus 4 GDI in 2014, came drive by wire, as the throttle cable was consigned to history. In 2008, this updated throttle-pedal arrangement kept the original look of the roller pedal, however the current throttle pedal is a very modern-looking black plastic item that can't easily be made into an organ pedal, although this could be done with a bit of engineering design. On some Morgans, drive by wire has proved to have a very sharp throttle response, which some owners have taken time to adapt to. The brake and clutch pedals are floor mounted, so their

arc of operation is almost horizontal, rather than the arc of conventional top-mounted pedals, which press down and away from the driver. Most drivers will adapt to this arrangement quite quickly.

IN CONCLUSION

This chapter is not meant to be an exhaustive list of what can be done by the enthusiastic owner, or home mechanic. Nor is it an exhaustive list of what is available from dealers and specialists. Browsing the Morgan Motor Co. and dealer websites, and the specialist websites, will provide a full picture of the Morgan accessories currently available – and the range continues to grow!

CHAPTER THREE

KEEPING THE RAIN OUT

It is probably true to say that modern convertible cars with modern hoods (soft-tops) and state-of-the-art seals don't usually leak when the weather turns wet, at least not when new. It is also probably true to say that many traditional Morgans do leak to some extent, and some more than others. I'm very pleased to say that our 2016 Plus 4 with an easy-up hood has so far proved to be 99.5 per cent watertight, even in monsoon conditions on the motorway – and most journeys in this Morgan have so far seemed to end up in heavy rain at some point.

THE TRADITIONAL STUDDED HOOD

The standard traditional hood simply wraps over the windscreen header rail and is held in place by nine lift-the-dot fasteners across the header; older

cars have ten fasteners. Wet weather can, and will, penetrate the lift-the-dot fasteners, and water will also be forced up the windscreen when in motion, where it will then force its way between the hood and screen header rail, and eventually drip down on to the legs of the occupants. This is why towels are such a good travel accessory when touring (*see* Chapter 12).

This hood design includes a full width, small diameter, padded roll of hood material that locates just behind the header rail, and is intended to resist the ingress of water. How effective this will be, depends on the position of the roll relative to the windscreen frame, and the tension of the hood fabric over the windscreen frame. The standard traditional hood with standard pivot points on the B panels doesn't provide for any adjustment. However, there are two possibilities for tightening this style of hood.

Two traditional studded hoods with clearly visible lift-the-dot fasteners on the screen header. The third car is an easy-up hood, and the visible header rail is the obvious difference.

Bear in mind, too, that a long journey with the hood raised at speed will stretch the Everflex, so on arrival at your destination you should expect to see some bagginess across the top of the hood. This will self-correct over time as the hood material shrinks back to normal. This effect is caused by the fabric ballooning, due to the air pressure inside the car. Opening a window slightly will help to reduce the pressure, but observe any convertible car with the hood raised at speed on the motorway, and you will notice the balloon effect.

To further reduce the ingress of water, it is possible to add some extra sealing to the front edge of the traditional studded hood, using flat-section, 4mm, soft (standard-density), closed-cell neoprene, and a narrow adhesive strip of neoprene profile, just above the lift-the-dot fasteners on the inside surface. This modification, along with re-tensioning the hood material as detailed below, can make a huge difference in keeping drips of water at bay, and adds some useful extra tension to the hood material.

A hood swivel pivot in the tensioned position but with the hood removed. To release the tension in the hood the handle (partly hidden behind the seat) rotates around the blue nylock nut, anti-clockwise from that position through approximately 180 degrees.

TENSIONING THE HOOD

My first suggestion for further tensioning the traditional hood comes from John Taylor of Phoenix Designs. John designed his hood-frame swivel pivots, and introduced them at the Cheltenham Morgan festival in 2001. These items replace the traditional studded hood-frame pivots on the B panels with an over-centre lever arrangement, using the original holes in the ash frame. This modification is therefore a very simple DIY improvement. The primary benefit is that the swivel pivots take the tension out of the hood when raising or lowering it, which makes it much easier to fasten, or unfasten the lift-the-dots across the screen header rail.

The swivel pivots are simple to both fit and operate. Before long I had obtained a pair for my 2012 4/4 Anniversary, which has the traditional studded hood in Everflex. When lowering the traditional studded hood, most owners will start by unfastening the rear, and when raising it, they will start by fastening the front of the hood on to the screen frame and will finish at the rear. However, when using the swivel pivots, you may find it easier when raising the hood,

to fasten the rear of the hood first, then to attach the hood fabric to the frame, and finally the front lift-the-dots to the screen frame, before re-tensioning the hood using the swivel pivots.

As the swivel pivots go over-centre into the taut position, they momentarily add extra tension to the hood fabric. In order to benefit from this feature, it is possible to drill the pivot mounting brackets, and add a small nut and bolt on each side to act as a stop. This modification means that the pivots will no longer move fully into their original tension position because the extra stop will hold them slightly away from this position, thus increasing the hood tension. You may also add tension to the hood fabric by sleeving the hood frame along the horizontal sections. For this, the solution is to use plastic adhesive tape or a plastic or sponge tube, which will remain attached to the hood frame. Even a small increase in frame diameter will add some extra tension to the hood fabric.

Finally, on the subject of the hood frame, to help prevent the fabric straps that wrap around the frame sections from moving sideways out of place, wind some electrical adhesive PVC tape around the frame on each side of the straps. This will hold them in place. Some owners also use a simple elastic strap to hold the hood frame in place when fitting the hood material over it. This arrangement hooks around the hood frame, and temporarily locates over the studs on the screen header rail. When the hood material has been partially located, the elastic strap can be taken off.

Around the rear of the traditional hood, there may be a few gaps between the hood fabric and the rear panel, especially at the corners. Here you can add a flat strip of 4mm standard-density neoprene, cut around the durable-dot fasteners, and stuck to the hood with contact adhesive. This will seal the gap quite well, and will reduce draughts from the rear.

THE EASY-UP HOOD

The easy-up hood, which was introduced as an option in 2003, is much more resistant to leaks than the traditional studded hood, but may still leak over the header rail. Inside the inverted U-shaped header rail, which is part of the hood frame, there is a ridged seal. This seal has evolved over time, and on later cars has a lip on each side, but is less developed on the earlier cars fitted with this hood. When this seal admits water, the water will usually drip from the sun

visor fixings, where the header rail is cut away, or at the very ends of the header rail.

This seal can be improved from a DIY perspective by adding a small, round-section neoprene profile (2 or 3mm) under the outer lip of the header rail; once guided in, it will remain there without adhesive and better resists the water, which is forced up the screen and under the hood header rail. If this modification doesn't do the trick, then a second neoprene profile may be added under the inner lip of the seal. On earlier cars it may be beneficial to replace the whole seal with the later version, so if you do have a leak here, consult your dealer.

In a small number of cases, the fixing brackets to the header rail will have broken at the welds, and so the hood frame should be treated with care and not put under too much strain. In 2013, Morgan Motor Co. added a C-profile, vertical A-post (or A-pillar) seal, which holds the sidescreen frames in place and resists water creeping round the A posts. They also added a robust sponge seal at each corner of the header rail, which locates on top of the A posts when the hood is raised.

Earlier cars with easy-up hoods don't have these features, but you may source them from your dealer, or sort out a similar DIY solution. Where the new seals at each end of the header rail don't prevent

The S-shaped A-post top seal, and the seal between the A post and sidescreen frame: 4mm standard-density neoprene on the top, and high-density polyethylene foam (HDPF) for the main seal, which came with a convenient and suitably angled edge.

The top of the offside A post. The seal facing the camera is the factory seal. To the right, the seal on the rear-facing surface of the A post is a neoprene addition. The S-shaped neoprene seal is visible between the A post and the header rail.

The same location, but now with a small triangle of mohair stuck to the header rail.

The current factory A-post top seal (the grey sponge) on the easy-up hood. The over-centre catch is to the left of this.

The factory A-post seal fitted to current cars, and which can be retrofitted to earlier cars.

The Sidescreen Window Channels

A build-up of rainwater in the sliding window channels is very likely in heavy rain, and this can then spill over into the interior. More recently, Morgan Motor Co. have drilled the lower front corner of the sidescreen frames, to allow the rainwater to drain away to the outside. Before this was done, on earlier Morgans, some dealers drilled a small hole in the front bottom corner of the perspex to achieve the same result, and this modification can easily be done at home using a small drill bit and a slow speed.

Another option is to fit an L-shaped neoprene profile into the window channel alongside the rearmost side window. This doesn't affect the slid-ing forward of the window, but it does limit how much rainwater can accumulate in the channel, and prevents it overflowing into the interior.

Rain may also get in where the top edges of the doors meet the sidescreens. In heavy rain and when the car is travelling at speed, water is forced upwards, partly by the shape of the door mirror bases, and it will bubble around the two vertical frame members that hold the sidescreens in place. To prevent this happening, cut and fold some carefully shaped pieces of soft neoprene sheet, and secure them to the frames in a suitable position using double-sided tape

The orange arrow shows an L-shaped seal added to the window channel, which is secured at each end with double-sided tape.

Folded and glued neoprene is secured with double-sided tape, and prevents water blowing up around the bracket. Although this appears to be a complex shape, it is a simple turnover, which is then trimmed at each end. Pressure between the sidescreen and door forces the seal into a permanent shape.

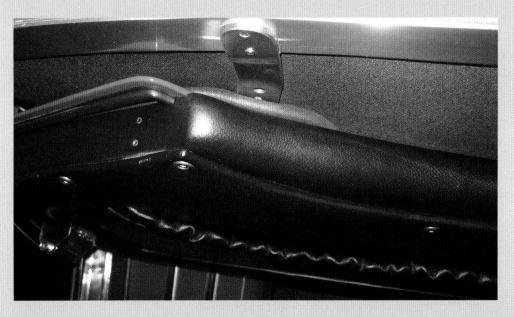

How the seal looks when the sidescreen is fitted.

leakage, then an additional 4mm neoprene pad may be added to the top of each A post.

Before these options were available from the factory, I added a neoprene S-section pad to the top of each A post on my 2005 Roadster, and I also added some A-post vertical seals, which just protrude into the airflow. The idea was to deflect the water away and prevent it from seeping around the inside of the sidescreen frames where they contact the A posts. In the top front corner of the hood I added a small triangle of mohair, which fills a small gap where rain might penetrate.

The rear section of the easy-up hood is well sealed against the rear panel, and doesn't appear to be prone to leaks. It is important to keep the two rear 'bonnet catches' lubricated and properly adjusted. Note that in use they may become slightly bent, so do take extra care if they need adjusting, because they may then stick. They are best adjusted by one full turn, but don't overtighten them or they may prove very difficult to release.

Access on cars with a spare wheel is simple enough (with some mild contortion), through the spare-wheel cavity in the rear panel. It is very important to press down on the rear hood frame when pulling the hood release handle, and not to be too heavy-handed when pressing the rear frame down to lock it in place. Occasionally the rear frame on earlier easy-up hoods has been known to fracture. With the hood stowed, you have the option of not locking the rear hood frame into the rear panel. With the hood cover or tonneau cover in place, it will need extra effort to lock and unlock, and the folded frame will lie on the rear panel unsecured without a problem.

When using a Morgan in bad weather, the slip-stream will leave a grimy residue around the rear seal of the easy-up hood. It's important to clean this off after a wet journey, because if left untouched, it has the potential to rub the paint over time. The traditional studded hood doesn't have a rear seal due to the overlap of hood material on to the rear panel, and in the three years we used one, often in wet weather, there was never a trace of road grime around the rear. This is probably due to the fit being rather gappy and so allowing some ventilation, which will prevent a low pressure area developing, and therefore dirt will not be sucked into that area.

At the sides, the design of both types of hood is such that, with a deep overlap of hood material over the sidescreen frames, water doesn't seem to penetrate at that point, although you must ensure that the hood material is properly located over the sidescreens. This is easy to overlook, especially with a passenger who doesn't know the arrangements, and Morgans do sometimes appear in photographs with the hood material trapped behind the sidescreen frame.

You may find that on older hoods, the stitching becomes porous, and this allows a damp patch to develop inside, which may extend along both sides of the hood, above the sidescreens. When this happens you can reproof the material, for which process a number of products is available. I've heard of beeswax being used for an Everflex hood, and there are several outdoor camping treatments available that will reproof the stitching.

Mohair needs a treatment that won't leave a stain, and one of the market leaders is Renovo, who supply cleaner, conditioner and reprofiler for mohair hoods. They also supply a well regarded, rear plastic window treatment to eliminate hazing and minor scratches. The plastic rear window panels are easily damaged, and so care should be taken, especially when folding the studded hood. Make sure it is stored where it won't rub against anything that might damage the plastic windows. The easy-up single rear window is much better protected, but take care that any hood material that is folded into the window area won't damage the plastic.

OTHER LEAKS

UNDER THE DASHBOARD

Very occasionally you might discover a drip or two of water from under the dashboard. This will be coming either from around the wiper spindles or the washer jets, or from rainwater that gets in through the louvres and penetrates the bulkhead. This type of leak can be very difficult to locate, and so will need a systematic check. Use a dropper around the wiper spindles and washers, and inspect under the dashboard using a torch. Seal up all the visible holes in the bulkhead, using grommets if possible, or sealer if not.

The dashboard is held in place with three or four wood screws, and with these removed, it may be eased forwards from the top, to allow inspection with a torch. This is easier with the steering column set low. Occasionally the windscreen washer tubes may leak, so if you have cause to look behind the dash, check these tubes at the same time. They can slip off the jets, or split, and either of these problems might cause screenwash to drip on to the electrics, which must be avoided at all costs. The washer tubes are delicate, but can be replaced if necessary with more robust tubes.

LEAKING TONNEAU COVER

Where a Morgan is left out in the rain with the full tonneau cover fitted, you should expect to find some leakage through the zip. This will be worse if the tonneau cover is slack, and if rainwater pools in the centre. Where possible, try to arrange the seats and head restraints so that the shape of the tonneau cover is more tent-like, allowing the rainwater to run off. Some owners have added a flap over the centre zip to reduce the likelihood of rainwater getting in.

DRYING THINGS OFF!

All the above suggestions should keep out most of the rain, although with any soft-top car it will always be a work in progress. If your Morgan does get wet inside, dry it off as much as possible at the end of your journey, and then leave it in a dry garage with the hood down. Use a dehumidifier or desiccant crystals if necessary. Some leathers will watermark, so you might also need to apply some leather conditioner and cleaner when the interior has dried out. Don't forget to check under the carpets, and if your Morgan gets wet often, then you should find some time to inspect under the inner sill, leather trim panels.

MISTING UP OF THE INSTRUMENTS

One question that is frequently asked by many new Morgan owners concerns misting and condensation inside the instruments – however, most Morgans do this to some degree. Smaller gauges seem to mist up much more than larger ones, and the problem can be much worse in cold weather – and there is no guaranteed solution. Some owners have drilled the instrument casing behind the dash to allow better ventilation. I have tried applying some clear plastic film on to the glass to see if extra insulation would help, but it didn't make much difference. Thankfully the misting will clear overnight, even after a cold day when some of the instruments become almost unreadable, and have visible droplets of water on the inside of the glass. However, they all do this, and it is nothing to worry about.

CHAPTER FOUR

PROTECTING THE WINGS AND BODY TUB

MORGAN WINGS

Morgan wings have been 'Superformed' in aluminium since late in 1997. The initial CAD design used three pairs of sample 4/4 hand-formed wings, and at the outset these wings are said to have caused some clearance problems at the front when first test-fitted to a Plus 8, which had larger wheels and tyres. The plan had been to roll the wing edges, but the aluminium proved to be too hard, which is what led to the U-shaped aluminium finisher being adopted along the wing edges.

A few years ago I was very fortunate in being able to visit Superform with a group of Morgan enthusiasts from the Talk Morgan forum, to see the process up close. The Superform design team, who manufacture many other aluminium panels for a variety of applications, are very well served by a sophisticated computer-aided 3D design programme. This software can take a virtual sheet of aluminium of specified thickness, and project a 3D image of how the finished panel will look after forming. It displays a coloured 3D contour graphic to show the resulting thickness of the

The wing fitting stage in the body shop. The black metal jig, which is used to get the correct panel alignment, will soon be removed so the cowl and radiator may be fitted. The over-rider brackets are loosely fitted at this stage, and no holes are drilled for the indicators.

aluminium, which will vary from how it began, as the uniform thickness flat sheet is stretched and moulded over the designated former using heat and compressed air.

This process forms two front, or two rear wings from a single piece of aluminium, which is then cut down the middle to form a pair. These wings are strong, and feature an aluminium U-shaped finisher, which is bonded on to the edge of each wing using a special adhesive. To the uninitiated, this finisher looks to be part of the wing panel. The headlamp bowls are spun aluminium, and these are TIG welded on to the wings.

At the point of fitting the wings to each new Morgan in the body shop, the wing blanks are trimmed along the inside edge according to the model and the wheel width. This is a highly skilled job, and the craftsmen make it look very easy, but it is not!

PAINT PROTECTION FILM

Paint protection film is available as an extra cost option on new-builds, and is 'invisibly' applied over forward-facing areas of the front and rear wings, around the edge of the cowl, and along the running boards. This option is well worth considering, as the forward-facing areas of the wings are vulnerable to stone chips, and the running boards are susceptible to scuffs from careless shoes, especially those of passengers! The clear coating is applied by specialist technicians in the paint finishing bay under strong lights, and is almost invisible. From a metre or so away, it is totally undetectable.

This film can also be applied to used cars, but the result will vary according to the existing paint condition, because it needs a blemish-free surface to fit invisibly. The film is impossible to photograph clearly, but your Morgan dealer will be happy to talk you through this option, and may have a Morgan in stock which is so fitted that you can inspect. If you undertake a factory tour, you will probably be able to inspect a Morgan which has had the film applied, or you may be lucky enough to be able to watch the technicians in action in the finishing bay.

WING PROTECTORS

THE REAR WINGS

On assembly, Morgan Motor Co. fit impact-resisting adhesive pads under vulnerable parts of the front wings. But these wings are a single skin, and although they are very strong, they can be damaged by flying stones. An impact from a sharp stone flung up by the tyre can dent the wing from below and create what is known as 'starring'. This is a small protruding bump in the paint, which may show slight cracking around the point of impact. Fortunately there is an option that will reduce the likelihood of this happening. The task is to add underwing mudflaps, or perhaps better described as wing protectors.

My preferred material for these items is 4mm, high density, polyethylene foam (HDPF). This is a dense form of neoprene sheet with high tear resistance, which is easy to cut and very light. It is stiffer, and therefore more effective, when stuck to a backing sheet. This may be either aluminium sheet cut to size, or a good alternative is circuit board, which is equally suitable. Maplins supply a rectangular circuit board, which is just the right size without cutting, stiffer than aluminium sheet, and is also very light.

I'll consider the rear wings first, because they are the simplest to deal with. Behind each rear wheel is a horizontal wing stay, which is at exactly the right height and angle in relation to the wheels. To secure the wing protector to this stay, the best option without drilling is to use three repair or penny washers, and the appropriate nuts and bolts for each side. The first step is to establish the measurements of the width between the ash inner wing panel and the outer wing edge. This will vary according to the width of the wheels.

Next, determine how long you want the protector to be. Placing a straight-edge from the rear contact point of the tyre up to the rear edge of the wing will show how long this needs to be for total protection. However, the optimum length makes the protector very visible from the rear of the car, and you may wish to compromise slightly, and cut them a

The left-hand rear wheel arch. The black reinforcer is a circuit board, but could be aluminium sheet. The method of attachment by penny washers can be clearly seen.

The rear wing protector when fitted.

little shorter. At the top edge, the protector should just touch the underside of the wing. If desired, this can be extended further, and some owners have taken their wing protectors over the top of the rear wheel, and down the front edge of the rear wing. If you choose to do this, then additional fixings will be needed.

Once the measurements have been checked at least twice and finalized, cut the neoprene with a sharp knife, and stick the circuit board or aluminium backing plate to the neoprene protector using spray-on high-strength contact adhesive in a well ventilated area, and leave to dry.

The final part of this job is to test fit each one to the car. When satisfied with the fit, measure and mark the backing plate, and drill three holes, at M5 size. Two holes should be just above the wing stay, evenly spaced, and one hole just below, centrally positioned. The protector will then hang over the wing stay, using the upper two bolts and penny washers, and will be retained in place by the lower single, centrally positioned bolt and penny washer. It is worth taking time to ensure that each protector is at the same height when viewed from the rear.

Any style of fastener will do the job, but stainless allen-headed setscrews suit this application. The penny washers will look and locate better if cut and shaped spacers are used around the wing stays. Finally, the protectors look much more professional if the corners are rounded off.

THE FRONT WINGS

Making front wing protectors is at the next level of complexity. Fortunately, the front wings have a pair of stays on each side, and the upper stays are roughly in the right position, but not at the right angle for a simple fix. This means that the fixing brackets here must be bespoke, and made up at the right angle to fit the stay, and also to provide the correct alignment for the wing protector. A little more ingenuity will be needed for this, because it is better not to drill the stays, but to devise a penny washer and bracket solution.

Due to the position of the stays, the protectors must be fixed low down, but will also locate behind the side indicator lamp units, which will prevent the protectors moving forwards at the top. Again, it is necessary to take careful measurements to obtain

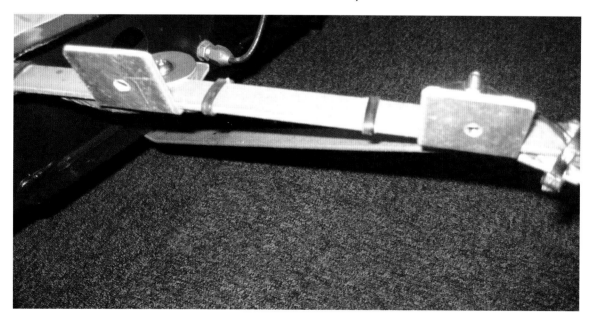

The two aluminium brackets (2mm thick) fastened to the upper front wing stay using penny washers. Note that on this Morgan the stays are reasonably close to horizontal. The angle of the brackets is a process of trial and error.

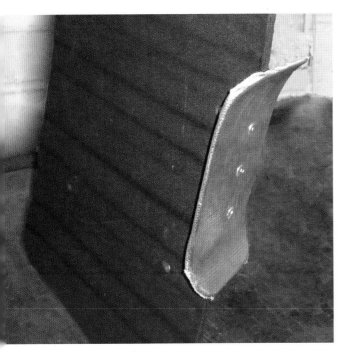

The Plus 4 offside (right side) wing protector. Because this is close to the exhaust, there is also a deflector plate covered in heat-resistant foil.

The wing protector from the rear looking forwards. Note the aluminium brackets on to the wing stay, and the heat-resistant weave, and the deflector plate.

The front nearside wing protector when completed. The side indicator repeater prevents the protector moving forwards.

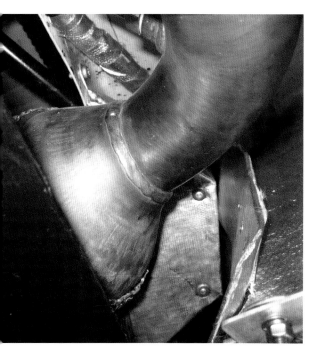

ABOVE: *A close-up view from under the exhaust. To the right is the deflector plate, and the heat-resistant foil. The wiring (top centre) is protected with an insulated sleeve. The steering column is upper left, and the box attached to the inner wing valance through which it passes, is lower centre right.*

RIGHT: *The front nearside protector on a Roadster showing the heat-resistant weave applied to the rear, and also the two angled brackets fixed to the wing stay.*

the best fit, and to use a backing plate of aluminium or circuit board to add strength and rigidity. You may choose to restrict the width of these wing protectors to the approximate front tyre width, although on 4-cylinder cars there is the option of going wide enough to reach the inner wing valance on the side of the Morgan without an exhaust.

Where the exhaust passes close behind the protector, for additional safety consider adding some woven reflective heat-resistant material, which may be glued to the back, but will also be held by the bracket fasteners.

On the current (2016) Plus 4, where the exhaust and catalytic converter pass very close, it will be necessary to cut away the wing protector, and add an aluminium deflector plate for extra protection. On the Duratec-engined Plus 4, the catalytic converter is situated under the offside (right side) front wing, and this can become very hot after a spirited drive. Insulated wraps are available for catalytic converters, and one of these is worth fitting as it will keep the front wing area much cooler after a long journey; it will also keep the catalytic converter at optimum temperature in cold and wet weather.

A neoprene shield fitted to the rear edge of the running board, and cut away to allow clearance for the exhaust. If there is no exhaust, then the protector may extend right across the panel.

THE RUNNING BOARDS

At the rear end of the front wing running boards there is a small vertical panel. Through this panel, on each side, pass two allen-headed set-screws, inserted from inside the front edge of the rear wing. Between the rear edge of the running boards and the rear wings are two rubber spacer washers, through which these set-screws pass. This vertical panel is bombarded by stones from the front wheels, but can be simply protected with a shaped piece of neoprene. There is sufficient exposed thread available on the fasteners to allow a penny washer and additional nut on each fastener to secure this neoprene protector without disturbing the originals. This protector must be cut away to allow sufficient clearance around the exhaust pipe.

Tread Rubbers

Some Morgans have tread rubbers fitted to the running boards. There can be up to three each side, although two is the most usual number. In the past, two tread rubbers were a standard fit, with an extra one being available at extra cost on wider running boards. In 2008, with the advent of the 4/4 Sport model, tread rubbers were no longer fitted as standard to that model. This approach then spread across the whole traditional range, and at the time of writing, no tread rubbers are standard, with an extra cost option for two per side.

The design of the tread rubber is very traditional, being a simple flat aluminium U channel with pointed ends, and a rubber filler strip. They are fixed to the wing by a series of miniature flat-headed steel coach bolts, with nuts and washers underneath the running board. The coach bolts are held in place by a square

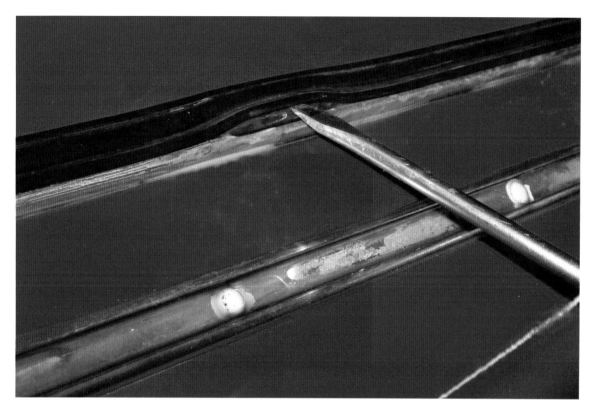

The screwdriver is for the purpose of illustration only. The rubber strip should come out using finger pressure only. The tread rubber channel, which is nearest, has had the bolt heads treated and painted. Use the edge of a credit card to refit the rubber.

section on the head, which locates in a matched hole in the aluminium channel.

As you might expect, these small square holes are easily rounded off, and this makes it more difficult to remove the fasteners. Eventually the coach bolts will corrode, and they produce a powdery rusty deposit on the heads, which show up by a series of regular humps in the rubber filler strip. These filler strips can be popped out quite easily, and even on recent cars it is a good idea to pop the rubbers out and apply some rust-inhibiting fluid over the bolt heads. If rust is visible, then use a fibreglass pencil or abrasive paper (carefully) to clean up the bolt heads. Then apply a dab of etch primer with a small brush, leave to dry, and finally cover with a rust-preventive fluid such as 3-in-1 oil, ACF-50, or Tectyl 506. Other products are available to do this.

In bad cases of corrosion of the heads, or when you suspect corrosion around the holes in the running boards, it may be necessary to remove the tread rubbers completely. This requires every nut to be removed from underneath, and so this becomes a slow and tedious job. One or both sides will have a silencer in the way, but with small hands and some patience and dexterity, it is possible to remove all the nuts without disturbing the silencer – though clearly this job will be much easier with it out of the way!

Replacing the rubbers into the aluminium channel is made easier with some light lubrication such as a quick detailer spray. Use the edge of a credit card to relocate the rubber under the aluminium lip, starting with both ends first, before working the rubber in towards the centre. Plastic or stainless fasteners may be used as a substitute for a longer-lasting solution.

WING BEADING

The factory handbook recommends that the wing beading is lubricated at least annually using 3-in-1 oil. Other specialist fluids are available, but bear in mind that the alternatives might affect the beading in the longer term. When doing this job, I transfer the fluid into a plastic container and feed it into the beading using a small artist's brush. A small eye dropper also works well. The liquid wicks into the gap very easily – and remember to do both above and below the beading. If road grime accumulates over time on each side of the beading, it can be removed by using a microfibre cloth folded over a credit card using quick detailer as a lubricant. This will reach right into the gap between the beading and body panels without damaging the paint.

THE FLEXING CHASSIS

The flexible nature of the chassis means that in normal use there will be a tiny amount of movement between the doors and the body tub. Where there is paint-to-paint contact, over time the paint will be rubbed away, eventually down to bare aluminium. The doors are fitted with rubber weather seals, but sometimes this is not enough protection for the paint. Every Morgan is different, and my 2005 Roadster does not suffer from any rubbing around the doors. But some Morgans do suffer from rubbing, and this can appear anywhere around the body tub where the closed door is a tight fit.

Prevention is better than cure, and so you might wish to add some paint protection film in the following places: along the top front edge of the bulkhead

This slightly grainy image shows how a tight-fitting door will rub the body tub. This was after 19,000km (12,000 miles), and the corresponding part of the door bottom was also rubbed to bare metal. The rubber seal on the door had been over-compressed by the tight fit.

The self-adhesive foil 'temporary repair': it is resistant to wear, and is better than repainting the panel, which might be slightly off colour, and may still abrade over time.

below the door beading; on the front upper corner of the door, where the sidescreen trim panel touches; on the body tub along the bottom edge of the door shut; and on the B post panel where the sidescreens fit when the door is closed. If your Morgan suffers from rubbing in these areas, it may be unwelcome, but it isn't serious, and it doesn't show from the outside with the doors closed.

Limited adjustment of the doors is possible, and the door lock can be eased out on the B post by loosening the bolts. However, if rubbing appears at the hinge end, this is much trickier to deal with, but is much more unusual, although I have seen this on one car recently. Self-adhesive neoprene weather seals are available, and these can be used to space

out the clearance between the door and body tub. Sometimes it is all about trial and error!

Where you face such an area of abrasion, there is really no point in having the panel repainted unless you can fix the cause. In the example shown in the photograph, a short-term solution was to apply yellow PVC electrical tape over the damaged area. I eased the door by adjusting the lock, and added extra weather seal under the door edge, and touched up the paint on the inside of the door. As a longer-term solution, I covered the body-tub damage with self-adhesive heat-resistant woven foil, which looked acceptable. The alternative was to risk a mismatched area of paint on the tub, and the 'temporary repair' is not visible from the outside with the door closed.

Wing Fasteners

In 2005, and previously, the front wings were secured with a mixture of fasteners. The section from the cowl to the bulkhead was held with allen-headed set-screws through the top edge of the inner wing valances, with conventional nuts underneath. On later Morgans these were changed to rivet nuts. A rivet nut is a threaded, rivet-shaped nut with a serrated outer edge that grips the panel, and behaves like a captive nut. These set-screws should be checked occasionally, as they do sometimes work loose. Under the body tub, the running-board section of the front wings was fastened with regularly spaced screws into the body.

At some point after this, an alternative method was tried with shaped securing brackets fitted to the tub, presumably to aid and speed up the assembly process. Further changes were made, and the current version has two L-shaped brackets with rubber buffers.

Also in 2005, the standard underseal was a brown or honey-coloured wax, probably Dinitrol 2000A or 4942. This was subsequently changed to black Dinitrol 4941, which is very good at inhibiting corrosion, very easy to touch up, and is available on-line in aerosol cans. However, this substance is quite unpleasant if you need to do any work where it has been applied, because it gets everywhere!

The limited edition ARP4 came with a clear underseal, so that the red chassis would remain visible. When I placed my order, I managed to persuade Morgan to use the same clear underseal on my Plus 4, because I much prefer the clear product, especially in the spare wheel well. The rear wings are attached to the body tub with a series of fasteners around the inner edge, and again, these should be checked occasionally for tightness.

Without wing protectors, the rear wings in particular will be blasted with road grit, especially at the rear, and over time this will remove the underseal and the paint – so this area, the lower few inches of each rear wing, should be inspected periodically and made good. All the weathering under a Morgan occurs beneath the wings. The good news is that for some reason, the centre tub section of chassis and floorboards will remain almost untouched by the weather, and stays remarkably clean.

The method of fitting the front wings in 2005. Note the regularly spaced fasteners into the body tub. At upper left, some tread rubber bolt tails with nuts are visible. Note also the non-standard insulated sleeve added over the fuel lines.

The current (2016) method of fitting the front wing: the first bracket (centre top) is secured in four places, while the second L-shaped bracket is secured with three set-screws and two wood screws. The opening in the front edge is best closed off with a neoprene bung.

The offside with the exhaust temporarily removed in order to access the fuel lines, and add reflective insulation material to them. A neoprene plug has been fitted into the end of the wing retaining bracket.

CHAPTER FIVE

THE REAR PANEL, VALANCE AND SPARE-WHEEL WELL

THE REAR PANEL

Over the years, the rear panel has displayed a number of badge variations. Sometimes there will be no badge, but you might find the 'Morgan' script or the model name, be it '4/4', 'Plus 4', 'Plus 8' or 'Roadster'. There may be a limited-edition model name. Usually these factory-fitted badges will be on the left side, and normally they have threaded studs that locate into holes in the panel. Sport models have the Morgan wings in the centre of the panel.

Because some owners will have added badges, you should expect some variation between cars, even from the same year of manufacture. The filler

cap on all the modern Morgans is on the right side, although very occasionally a new-build will emerge with a dummy filler on the left-hand side as a special order. At the time of writing, Morgan Motor Co. are not quite as receptive to unlisted special requests as they once were, which is a shame!

THE SPORT MODELS

You might think, when looking at the inclined rear panel of your modern two-seater traditional Morgan, that there wasn't much scope for improvement. If you have chosen a Sport version or limited edition model without a spare wheel, then you would be pretty much correct – unless you have a circular

Awaiting a road test, a left-hand-drive 1600 4/4 Sport. Originally the 4/4 Sport had thin rear reflectors mounted under the edge of the rear wings, with earlier larger reversing and fog warning lights. Before long, the reflectors were changed to these, by Maxparts, across the range.

removable panel through which there is access into what lies beneath, like the limited edition ARP4.

With the Sport models, aside from having the option of fitting a luggage carrier or rack, which then provides a further option of adding a spare wheel on top of the rack, there's little more that can be done in this area. But most bespoke traditional Morgans are fitted at the factory with a spare wheel, and this does provide a few more opportunities to take care of things.

THE REAR VALANCE

In 1997, full bumpers were the standard fit on new Morgans (no doubt with an exception or two). From mid-1997, the bumpers were stainless steel, and the bumper ends were enclosed to satisfy new safety regulations. The rear valance was a vertical panel with tapered ends on to which the rear number plate was affixed, with a standard Lucas L467 lamp at each end for illumination. The L921 reversing light and fog warning light were mounted separately above the rear bumper.

Over time, the rear number plate was raised to bumper height, with a revised rear panel. Some

Morgans from this era (1997–2002) now have the reversing light and fog warning light fitted below the bumper. This may have been done at a later date by a dealer or owner. An aftermarket stainless-steel number-plate box is available which fixes over the bumper, and can also be fitted at the front. Often owners have lowered the rear number plate to the earlier position for aesthetic reasons, and so you should expect some variation on Morgans from this period.

In 2002, Morgan Motor Co. built a limited edition of eighty Le Mans '62 (LM62) celebration cars. Forty of these were 4/4 models, and forty were Plus 8s. These cars were fitted with stainless-steel over-riders, and a front number-plate box with a short undertray, formed from aluminium. The new design of over-rider was very different to the earlier versions used by Morgan at the rear, and look identical to those fitted to the rear of the Austin-Healey Sprite. However, the brackets welded inside are different, and the Morgan version has a hole and bracket on the bottom edge. The hole is covered with a rubber grommet. The front number-plate box was later produced in acrylic

A 1997 two-tone Plus 4, showing the standard rear valance at that time. This is one of the last short-door Plus 4s, but you would be hard pressed to tell from this angle.
JOHN HAYES

The current production rear number-plate panel and valance, with suspended fog warning light and reversing light. The reflectors were changed from rectangular to circular around 2008. JOHN STRIDE

for standard production Morgans, which had the optional over-riders fitted from that year.

At the same time, a new rear valance was required for the over-rider equipped cars. This is a simple curved acrylic closing panel, and is fixed to the body-tub frame by self-tapping screws, and into the rear chassis crossmember by small nuts and set-screws. This panel carries the L794 reversing light and L795 fog warning light, and over the past twenty years has evolved further. Whether each Morgan has full bumpers, over-riders, or neither, and the year of build, will determine the specification of the rear panel. With neither fitted, or with over-riders fitted, the valance panel carried the reversing and fog warning lights on black rubber plinths, which resemble the front indicator light plinths, but are not the same. At the rear, the lamp lenses were silicon sealed on to a coarse-threaded chrome bezel, which screws directly into the rubber plinth. The bulb fits from the rear when the lens is unscrewed, and these can be quite stiff to unscrew, and so are often not screwed fully home. The lenses (one white, one red) have two visible 'virtual fasteners': these are blind rivets that simply fill the unused holes in the lenses, and can be prised out easily with a small screwdriver. The blind rivets may be replaced with crossheaded screws, if you prefer the look of these.

This rear valance was redesigned, sometime in 2009, first by altering the shape of the number-plate backing plate by squaring off the ends, and then by adding two integrated raised holes, behind which smaller versions of the reversing light and fog warning light are fitted from the rear. Very occasionally these lamps may take in water, and the best way to remove the water is to remove the lamp unit, dry it out, and then drill a small drain hole in the bottom of the lens.

Where over-riders are fitted, or a luggage rack is fitted without over-riders, two elliptical holes must be cut in the rear valance so that the 'J'-shaped fixing brackets, or rack mounting brackets, may pass through and locate in the ends of the chassis members, where they are secured with a pair of fasteners on each side. Access to these fasteners is tight. The holes in the rear valance are usually quite tight against these brackets, but may be visually improved by adding some U-channel neoprene edging around the holes, to match the edging fitted as standard around the front number-plate box fitted to cars with over-riders.

On the outer edges of the later rear valance are two moulded cut-outs. There is one each side, and these are made to allow access to the exhaust tailpipe mounting bracket on the chassis ends. They are usually manually opened up more on the side with the exhaust (so both sides on the Roadster). These holes can be covered to give a cleaner appearance, by fabricating an aluminium cover plate, painted to match the valance. The covers may be attached using double-sided tape, and as a final touch, U-channel neoprene edging

The earlier rear valance, with integral number-plate backing plate, larger reversing light and fog warning light on rubber plinths, and over-riders. Note that this number-plate backing plate has angled ends. The reflectors are rectangular with chrome bezels.

The later rear valance with the small Hella reversing light and fog warning light, and over-riders.

LEFT: *The standard later rear valance with squared-off ends, with the small reversing light and fog warning light, without over-riders.*

BELOW: *In final finish, June 2016, awaiting rear over-riders. Note that the holes are ready cut in the rear valance prior to painting. This image provides a good indication of where they should be situated if you wish to retrofit these brackets.*

A close-up of the later rear valance panel showing access cut out for the exhaust mounting. Note also the non-standard neoprene edging fitted around the over-rider bracket hole to the left.

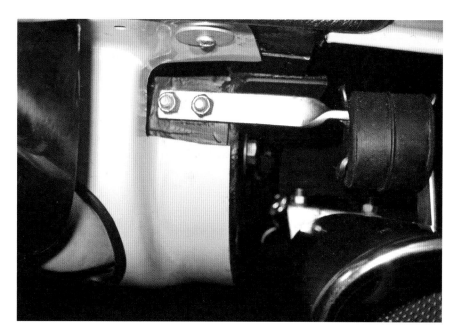

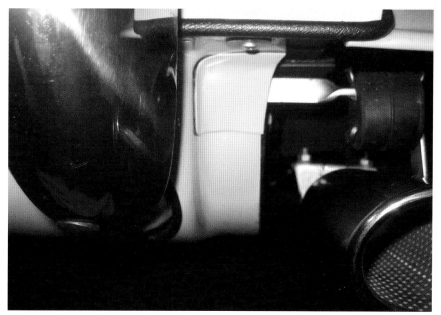

The same panel, now with an aluminium cover plate added.

can be added down each edge of the valance to give a matching finished look.

The rear number-plate lights are a standard item across the modern traditional Morgan range, but the number-plate backing plate has evolved in shape and is very different on cars with full rear bumpers, where the reversing light and fog warning light are still separate units mounted on to the rear bumper. Some owners have adapted their number-plate backing plate to mount the plate lower than the current factory position, in a style that was used by the factory back in the 1960s. The 'Cobra' high-level brake-light lens, which is fitted to all Morgans except the Sport models, is L760/L874, with number 7421 also showing on the lens.

The full rear bumper showing the separate rear number-plate backing plate, and separate reversing light and fog warning light. Note also how the luggage rack is attached to the bumper irons. This Morgan has a mohair spare-wheel cover. STEVE HARRIS

THE SPARE-WHEEL WELL

Lifting out the spare wheel for the first time can be something of a surprise. Where there is no luggage rack fitted, after unscrewing and removing the T bar, invariably the spare wheel will slide down, often suddenly, until it hits the bottom edge of the rear panel with a bump. It is good practice to pad out this space beforehand by inserting an old towel into the gap at the bottom.

If the 'Cobra' high-level brake light is fitted, lifting out the spare wheel cleanly takes a bit of practice, and the Roadster wheel in particular is heavy and unwieldy. This is due to the angle of location, and because you have to reach over the rear of the car to lift it out, take great care of your back when doing this, and don't put your fingers around the spokes, or trap them against the edge of the panel.

There is quite a simple solution to the sliding spare-wheel issue, and this comes from the Morgan factory woodshop offcuts box. On a factory tour, as you pass through the woodshop, you may be invited to help yourself to an offcut of wood from the scrap box. Often these offcuts come from the rear wheel-arch ply panel, created in the famous factory jig, and so are curved to match the wheel and tyre profile. With some effort with a saw and sandpaper it is possible to create a matched pair, with the right curve to match the spare-wheel tyre. With a bandsaw, it would also be possible to create similar pieces of wood from a solid block.

Located across the spare-wheel cavity there is an ash crossmember, quite close to the spare-wheel centreline, but just below it. This crossmember is a little higher than the ideal position, but is just about right for attaching the two curved pieces of ash ply.

The spare-wheel cavity, showing the triangular neoprene corner pads, and the curved retaining pieces of ash ply.

After working the offcuts, a matched pair of curved ash-ply pieces.

The curved retaining piece fitted, and also the thick masking on the panel edge, which is essential to avoid any damage from the drill.

This can be achieved by using two long crosshead screws on each side, and some wood glue. Ash is a hardwood, and drilling pilot holes takes time and care, but pilot holes are essential in hardwood – and for this job, it is important to measure at least twice! By carefully measuring the relative positions, the curved wood pieces will just touch the tyre at the eight o'clock and four o'clock positions.

Drilling pilot holes in the ash crossmember in the Morgan also needs exceptional care, because the chuck and body of the drill come very close indeed to the edge of the sloping rear panel, and this must be masked with multiple layers of masking tape. After completion, leave it to dry overnight, and then do a test fit. It may be necessary to add a strip of 4mm neoprene on each side to provide a cushion. When the spacing is right, the spare wheel will either be held in place, or will slide down very slightly when the T bar is removed. When replacing the spare wheel and refitting the T bar, the wheel will now be held in approximately the right position, and very little effort is involved in starting the T-bar thread.

Without this modification, it can be quite difficult to hold the spare wheel in place on the incline whilst inserting the T bar and starting the thread. Having a luggage rack to contend with, makes this even more difficult to achieve.

THE SPARE WHEEL FILLER

Once in position, the spare wheel rests on an inclined metal plate, and in order to provide some protection for the tyre sidewall, consider adding some neoprene sheet, cut into triangles and stuck down at each corner of the plate with contact adhesive.

If your spare wheel is a wire wheel, then unless you invest in a vinyl or mohair cover for the spare, you can see through the spokes into the spare-wheel well. This opening can be closed off by making up a circular panel to fit inside the wheel rim. Pre-cut acrylic circles can be ordered on-line, but these need very careful measurements so that the circle fits exactly around the wheel centre and inside the back of the wheel. This will close off the opening, and looks like an original part of the Morgan.

A yellow acrylic spare-wheel filler, held in place with two small neoprene wedges at the twelve o'clock and six o'clock positions.

A red acrylic filler panel fitted under the spare wheel. The 'R' clip that retains the crossbar above the sidescreen storage area is visible on the left. Some luggage racks have a knob on the end of the bar instead of an 'R' clip.

The acrylic can be supplied in a limited number of colours, and the red option is an excellent match for Corsa red. Other colours may need painting to match the Morgan. Spare-wheel covers are available from dealers and specialists in Everflex or mohair, either as a full cover, or as a tyre cover only with a transparent plastic centre to display the wire wheel.

When the spare wheel is off the Morgan, take the opportunity to check the tyre pressure. It is much harder to inflate the spare when fitted on to the Morgan, unless you have a 12-volt compressor. If you have only a foot pump, this can be achieved by placing a sheet of plywood on the spare wheel or the luggage rack, and using the foot pump on the wood, and pumping by hand. I usually set the spare pressure at +5psi over the recommended pressure to allow for some pressure loss over time.

THE FUEL-FILLER PIPE

The fuel-filler pipe is accessible to the right, in the spare wheel well. Earlier Morgans have a single T-piece rubber pipe, whereas later cars have an aluminium take-off just under the filler cap, and use two separate pipes. The thicker of the two is the main filler pipe to the fuel tank, and the smaller pipe is the vent pipe. The main pipe must be as straight as possible, and even with just a slight kink it can slow down the rate at which you can refuel. By loosening the lower worm-drive clip it takes only a few minutes to push the pipe down further on to the tank filler, and this eases the kink. Some owners have also found that a kink in the vent pipe has a similar effect, and so you should also check the thinner rubber pipe that attaches to the filler head, and make sure that this has no kinks.

The position of the sprung flap inside the filler cap may affect refuelling speed, and it seems that this is best with the hinge at the twelve o'clock position. The sprung flap can be repositioned by finger pressure, and it will spin round inside the filler neck. If this doesn't make a difference, it may be worth experimenting with the flap in different positions.

The single-piece fuel-filler hose used on earlier cars in this period. This can stiffen and perish as it ages. It carries the part number MPS0445, but the manufacturer is unknown.

The fuel-filler hose on a 2016 Morgan. If the hose is kinked it can be straightened by loosening the lower hose clip and pushing the hose further down on to the tank pipe. The thinner hose to the left is the vent from the tank, which should curve gently downwards.

RIGHT: *The sprung flap inside the fuel filler, which can be repositioned to improve the speed of filling.*

BELOW: *April 2017: this storage rack is in the finishing bay. On the upper shelf are eight dashboards: they all appear to be walnut except the one on the left, which may be burbinga. Below are a number of rear valances and front number-plate boxes.*

CHAPTER SIX

SELECTING AND FITTING ACCESSORIES

LUGGAGE RACK OPTIONS

A stainless-steel luggage carrier, or rack, is essential if you intend to take your Morgan on touring holidays. Although on initial examination they all look very similar, you need to be aware that the luggage racks currently available are not all to the same design, and on closer inspection, some are more pleasing to the eye than others. The first and major difference between them is that some luggage racks have a sidescreen storage facility under the luggage deck, and some do not. Luggage racks also vary around the 'T-bar' mounting, where some have a crossbar centred on the spare-wheel centre, whilst others are offset below that position.

The method of fixing, either to the full bumper, the over-riders, or neither, also varies by rack manufacturer. Some T bars are straight, and some have a slight 'V' shape to the handle, although the T bar, which secures the spare wheel, is already present on every Morgan built with a spare wheel.

Where a Morgan is fitted with a wider spare wheel, it may be necessary to fit an aluminium spacer, or tube, under the T-bar mounting. This will provide clearance between the rack crossbar and the spare-tyre sidewall at each side. Spacers are available in different thicknesses, and may be at extra cost, so you should ask your dealer or specialist.

Some luggage racks will need additional work on the over-rider brackets before fitting, by filing down

A 4/4 Sport with a standard factory luggage rack. This Morgan has had a modified hood fitted, similar to the factory easy-up; note that the three turnbuckles on the B panel are now no longer used. Note also the position of the high-level brake light on the Sport model. STEVE HARRIS

A Roadster Sport without over-riders, using the factory U-bar fixing, but also with the optional spare-wheel attachment and V-shaped T bar. The rear number-plate backing plate has square-cut ends. Note also the aftermarket rear-view mirror and door mirrors. STEVE HARRIS

A luggage rack with T-bar attachment in line with the crossmember. Note the R clip on the left, and the yellow acrylic spare-wheel filler. The quarter tonneau cover fitted here is bespoke. The rear-view mirror is aftermarket, but the door mirrors are the round factory items.

Another variation of the luggage rack. This has vertical stays down to the over-riders. Note also that the rack crossmember is below the T-bar fixing. This Morgan has an aftermarket rear-view mirror with round factory door mirrors. The hood cover is in place. STEVE HARRIS

The Librands brackets for 'no over-riders', with a 'Heart of England' rack without sidescreen storage. Where over-riders are not fitted, two holes must be cut in the rear valance in line with the ends of the chassis rails. This dashboard is Zebrano. PETER GILBERT

An alternative luggage-rack fixing solution without over-riders, and a rack without sidescreen storage. Note also that this Morgan Roadster has a narrow 4/4 size spare wheel. At the factory, June 2012. JOCHEN ERNSTING

the brackets along their top edges. This is so that the stainless luggage-rack brackets can be fitted squarely and properly. This job is basically hand finishing and therefore part of the Morgan experience, and so is a task that a competent home mechanic should manage. A power file will make the job much easier, but it can be completed with a simple hand file.

Some luggage racks attach to these brackets with standard stainless nuts and bolts, but this look may be improved with socket cap setscrews and domed nuts. One design of rack has vertical columns that slot into the over-rider brackets; with this design, once the T bar is removed, the rack will lift away.

When the luggage rack is fully loaded, the weight, vibration and chassis flex will put a strain on the nut and bolt rack fixings. Stainless fasteners can be brittle, and so it is good practice, where possible, to fit the rack legs on to the rear brackets such that, if the bolt shears, the rack leg will drop on to the bracket, rather than on to the rear panel.

SIDESCREEN STORAGE

Some versions of the luggage rack have a 'J'-shaped retainer on the centre rear crossbar to prevent the sidescreen bag slipping out. Racks with sidescreen storage have a removable cross tube, usually secured with an 'R' clip to the left, or by a knurled knob on the right-hand end of the cross tube. This feature allows the sidescreens, in their bag, to be slid into place.

The sidescreen bag has a centre partition so that the sidescreens don't rub against each other when being carried on the rack. The increase in their size from 1997 means that if you source a secondhand rack from before that change point, the post-1997 model sidescreens may not fit in the storage area. This is all quite complicated, and hopefully the photographs in this chapter will help to better illustrate some of the luggage rack options.

Racks are also available for the four-seater Morgan, and some of these have sidescreen storage. The four-seater racks are much closer to vertical, and some also have a drop-down section to provide a hori-zontal platform. They protrude some way behind the rear of the car and so must be loaded with care. A huge benefit to four-seater ownership is that when travelling two-up, your luggage can travel inside the car with the rear seats folded, and so is much better protected from the weather.

FITTING A REPLACEMENT BRAKE LIGHT

With luggage secured on the rack, the standard high-level brake light, or Cobra as it is sometimes known, may be obscured from the rear. The Sport model has a high-level brake light recessed into the top of the rear panel instead of the Cobra, and so this may be even more obscured if a luggage rack is fitted. Some owners have made up a replacement high-level brake light, either to fit on to the luggage, or to attach to the rearmost part of the luggage rack.

With the spare wheel removed, and with a measure of 12-volt electrical knowledge, it is simple enough to add a 12-volt supply from the base of the

Note the bespoke high-level brake light. The Morgan luggage set, which in 2008 was the American Tourister case plus mohair cover and Morgan-branded leather straps. Included in the set, and in front of the case, is a cylindrical boot bag that zips on to the mohair cover.

Cobra, with a plug on the end, to feed power to an additional high-level brake light. When so fitted, the plugged end of the supply wire can be fixed to lie just inside the rear panel when not in use, and can be retrieved easily when needed. The components to build such a replacement light are available from auto-electrical suppliers.

SPARE-WHEEL SECURITY

Depending on the design of the luggage rack and how it fits under the T bar, a metal cover may be designed and fitted over the T bar, to deter casual interference when the car is parked and unattended. Interference with Morgans when they are parked is rare, but there was one incident a few years ago when a spare wheel went missing overnight from a

hotel car park. A luggage rack over the spare wheel does make it harder to interfere with, but more can be done, and the obvious route to achieve this, is to cover the T bar with a metal protector.

This can be done by making a U-shaped cover plate from a rectangle of stainless steel or aluminium, then obtaining two U bolts of the right size, which must be drilled through, and bolted inside the cover. Next, cut out and drill a baseplate to fit under the luggage-rack cross tube and around the T-bar hole. The cover plate can be lined and edged with neoprene, and then secured with four washers and dome nuts from below. Being stainless steel, or aluminium, this looks original and completely covers the T bar.

This modification makes it more difficult and time-consuming to interfere with the spare wheel, without having the right size spanner. The cover-plate solu-

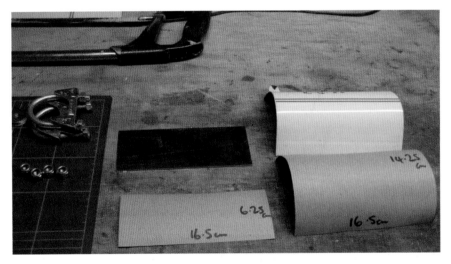

The base components of the spare-wheel protector. The cover, the baseplate and the U bolts, showing the measurements.

Drilling the masked-up and marked cover, before drilling through the U bolts. A pedestal drill would make this more accurate, and easier to do.

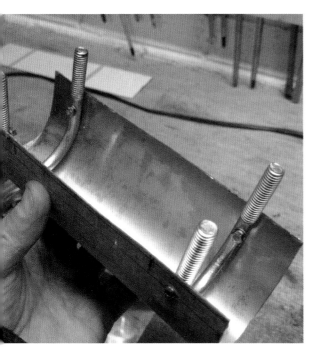

Now at the initial assembly stage: the basic T-bar cover with U bolts attached.

The edging has been added, and the baseplate is in the early stages of preparation.

A T-bar cover in mirror-finish stainless steel. The U bolts are secured with metal clips. The Roadster spare wheel uses a thick spacer, so it is necessary to bulge the cover to fit around the spacer.

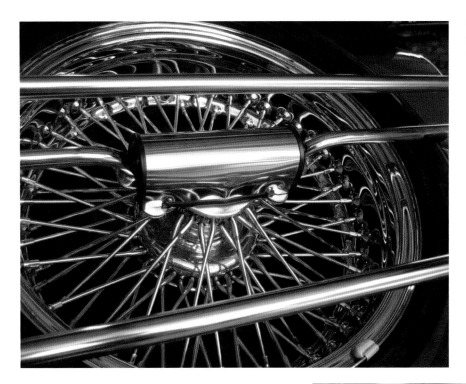

The mirror-finish cover when fitted to the Roadster.

tion doesn't work without a luggage rack, but it may be possible to devise something similar by drilling the aluminium spacer under the T bar, and fixing a threaded bar into the spare-wheel retaining bracket.

DOOR ACCESSORIES

DOOR MIRRORS

There are two standard types of door mirror available from the factory on new-builds. The earlier standard mirror is almost rectangular, with one edge slightly deeper than the other. This type of mirror has a limited range of adjustment, and has a poor field of view on the passenger side. The second type of standard mirror is circular and has a better field of view. The circular mirror option was introduced around 2008.

Replacement door mirrors are available from dealers and specialists, in stainless steel. There is a choice of either a pair of mirror heads to fit the existing bases, or a full replacement set, including the bases. There are at least four mirror designs with a similar variety with the shape of the stalks. All

The Morgan Motor Co. standard rectangular door mirrors.

provide more adjustment and a much improved field of view than the standard mirrors.

Changing these over is a simple job, and it is worth adding a neoprene buffer under the mirror base to prevent the internal spring damaging the paint beneath. Don't overtighten the screws, and use stainless screws if possible. Measure the required length

The Morgan Motor Co. optional round door mirror. These are sometimes fitted as the standard mirror on limited edition cars.

An aftermarket stainless mirror, including base, from 'Heart of England' Morgan. Compare the base to the standard factory item. The stainless base has an improved black sealing grommet at the stalk. Note also that the sidescreen Philips-headed screws have been capped.

An alternative aftermarket stainless mirror, including base. This mirror is slightly larger than the previous example, with a different stem but an identical base, again from 'Heart of England' Morgans.

carefully, and ensure a good seal to stop the ingress of water. The factory applies a silicon-type sealer to the door-mirror screws in order to make a good weatherproof seal.

Over the period covered by this book, Morgans were supplied new, with a large, dipping, black plastic rear-view mirror on the windscreen. Most owners soon replace this with a smaller classic non-dipping design, which has more recently been added to the options list by Morgan Motor Co. Two sizes of replacement rear-view mirror are available from dealers and specialists. (*See also* note in Chapter 2.)

DOOR CHECKS

The Librands door checks are popular and highly recommended. They are a polished, stainless-steel piece of engineering design, in a boomerang shape. They control door opening better than the factory leather straps, and will hold a door in the fully open position, making it much easier to get in and out without banging your legs. The bulkhead fixings for these are screwed into threaded holes in the underdash roll hoop, so once these holes are located, the setscrews will go straight in.

On the doors, the fasteners are wood screws, and more care is necessary to ensure that these screws are not longer than the door timber is thick! Misjudge this measurement, and you may push two pimples into the outer door skin. The two existing holes in each door frame may need a slight enlargement to accept the new screws, but if using a drill, use a slow speed and be really careful about the depth. You may wish to cut the ends off the screws, then you should measure twice to be certain that the screw won't reach the outer door skin.

OTHER USEFUL ACCESSORIES

SPOTLAMPS

Spotlamps are a very popular option, and were a standard fit on the Morgan Plus 8 for many years. The wiring may be already present in the loom, and on some models there is a spare switch on the dashboard, which on later cars is also used for air-conditioning,

The Librands door check in place, in the fully open position. The mounting brackets have been trimmed with small leather patches.

The Librands door check almost fully closed, with Union Flag trim. The brackets are trimmed with leather, secured with double-sided tape. Note also the leather-trimmed, steering-column cowl.

when fitted. The spotlamps may be fitted directly to the front of the wings, or to the front bumper. There is also a kit available to fit a small pair of spotlamps to brackets hidden inside the front number-plate box on Morgans with over-riders, although this option is quite rare. Always take professional advice if you are not familiar with fitting and wiring-in accessories.

WIND DEFLECTORS

Wind deflectors are available in perspex or in glass. They are 'trapezoid' in shape and locate on to the windscreen A posts. With the sidescreens stowed, these deflectors are positioned at a suitable angle to reduce the flow of air around the sides of the windscreen. Not everyone likes the look, and opinions vary as to whether they make much difference. One type fits outside the windscreen frame A post, and these will interfere with opening the doors when the sidescreens are in place.

There are two types of fixing bracket: the earlier cars have a flat A-post surface, and so the brackets are flat faced, while cars with the current A post need a curved bracket face. An alternative, more expensive glass version fits inside the A post and sidescreen frame, but it's not clear whether these can be made to fit the current A-post design. I would not wish to drill holes in the current A posts, so if you wish to fit these internally mounted wind deflectors, then seek expert advice.

SUN VISORS

Conventional sun visors, which match the interior trim, are an extra cost option on new-builds. The small threaded fixing tubes on the screen top frame are a standard fit, whether the Morgan has sun visors or not. Aftermarket visors are available in tinted perspex, although they are not widely advertised at the time of writing. However, tinted visors are available on-line for the classic Mini. These are slightly too narrow to fit the Morgan, but these visors do provide an inexpensive route to obtain the four chromed swivel brackets, which if sourced separately

Wind deflectors fitted to the flat-sided A pillars, which were standard fit with the studded hood. Special shaped deflectors can be fitted to folding windscreens. Note also the early version of the tilt/reclining seats, which are a very different shape to those that followed. GLENN BARKER

Glass wind deflectors fitted to the inside of the A pillars. Note also the sidescreen trim panel, the polished wood inlay and steering-column shroud, the aftermarket lock cover, door checks, and stainless B-post finisher. This short-door Morgan has demister vents at the base of the screen. STEVE LANGSTON

A close-up of grey-tinted perspex visors and an aftermarket rear-view mirror. These visors are semi-fixed in position. With the mounting brackets the other way round, the visors may be used conventionally.

are very expensive. The tinted perspex visors may be used conventionally, or with the brackets reversed may be used inclined upwards and semi-fixed. This does depend on how tall you are, because for taller owners, they may fall right within your eye line.

If you make up your own visors from scratch, then note that the distance from the outer edge of the visor to the screen frame is important, to allow the over-centre catches of the easy-up hood enough space to operate. This is not important if you have the traditional studded hood. The distance between the inner edge and rear-view mirror is also important if you intend to use perspex sun visors in the conventional manner, because the gap here is marginal.

THE WINDSTOP

Some owners have fitted a windstop behind the seats, but very few dealers offer a Morgan-specific product off the shelf. So you may choose to adapt one from another similar sized convertible, or make up your own. If you prefer not to drill holes into your Morgan, the best solution is to attach a windstop to the head-restraint columns. The disadvantage of this

option is that both seats must remain in the same position relative to each other. An alternative would be to attach some brackets on to the side of the rear wheel-arch panels, but this will require some drilling into the body frame.

After trial and error design work with cardboard templates, the optimum bracket design was achieved by using 2mm aluminium, cut out so that a head-restraint column would slide through, and with an angled face at the rear to attach to the perspex windstop. These brackets must be lightly padded using neoprene, and look best if covered with black leather. A metal finisher may be added around the head-restraint stalks, which is also used on the top of the seats. This finisher is available from MG specialists, as it was a standard British Leyland fitting. The next step is to fit these two brackets to the head-restraint stalks. The photographs will better explain how this works.

There are two variables. The first variable is the angle of bend of the bracket. The brackets rest on the top of the seat backrests, and in this position, the angled sections that attach to the perspex windstop must be close to vertical, so some last-minute

The first successful attempt at windstop brackets, using perspex and a stainless-steel L-shaped bracket.

The second version of the bracket: a single piece of aluminium, covered with leather, and using penny washers as spacers. This is with the tombstone head restraints.

The third version of the bracket, this time with the later, oval profile head restraints, which need fewer spacers. The perspex still has a protective film at this point.

The most recent version of the windstop brackets is to fit the sports performance seats, which require either a longer bracket, or long spacers.

This image shows the underside of the brackets, which are shaped and padded so that there is no abrasion to the top of the seats.

Here, the spacers have been trimmed, first with a mohair tube glued into place over the elongated nuts, and then with a leather tube glued over the mohair.

The bracket in position and ready to accept the perspex panel.

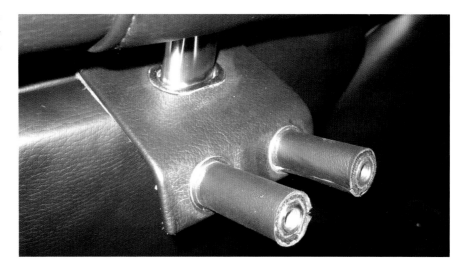

The bracket from the front.

Finally, the windstop is completed, with a neoprene C-edge trim added.

The most recent design of windstop, deeper than the one in the previous photograph. It has cut-outs for the seat belts, and is tinted light grey. This one looks better without edging.

adjustment by bending may be necessary. The second variable is the type of head restraint involved. Each one of the three, whether it be the tombstone, the oval type, or the sports performance head restraint, will require a different spacing.

It is easier to make the brackets roughly the right size and use spacers, than to attempt a perfect fitting bracket without spacers. There is an optimum thickness of spacers, at which point the windstop touches the back of the head restraints and stays vertical. Use penny washers, spacer washers, extended nuts and stainless fasteners to finish this job.

With the hood down, nothing will ever eliminate draughts in a Morgan, but this modification has worked well, and it does reduce back draughts. However, as already noted, the arrangement requires both seats to remain in the same relative position, which won't suit everybody. The overall size of perspex was initially trial and error, because I wanted the windstop to fit under the hood, should that be necessary. Laser-cut perspex is readily available on-line, and so once the design was finalized, it was simple to order a bespoke piece of tinted perspex, pre-drilled and with polished edges, ready to fit. The seat belts run underneath the windstop, and are unaffected.

THE PASSENGER TONNEAU COVER

Many owners who have the full tonneau cover find that it is not especially user friendly, as already mentioned in Chapter 1. However, despite being a challenge to fit and remove, the easy-up hood cover tidies up the look of the hood when it is folded. But the hood cover leaves an uncovered section behind the seats between the hood frames. This exposed area may be covered by cutting out a rectangular piece of mohair. At the rear edge it will need two holes to fit round the two rear hood-frame catches. At the front, it can be held in place by adding two mohair straps, which wrap around the hood frame under the hood cover, and use the existing dura-dots on the frames to fix into place. This is something that a professional trimmer could produce quite easily.

If you travel much on your own, it may also be worth considering making up a tonneau cover just for the passenger side. Again, this will need a piece of mohair to cover the space from the windscreen base back to the hood cover. But this piece of mohair is a complex shape, and a thick brown-paper template is the best place to start. If you don't want the unbalanced look of a single (driver's) head restraint with the tonneau cover in place, then add and trim a hole, so that the passenger head restraint can be left in place over the top of the tonneau cover.

To prevent excessive flapping of the unsecured edge, a fibreglass tent pole, or rod, may be adapted to fit down the centre of the cockpit, with padding at both ends. The passenger tonneau cover can be attached to this, using mohair tabs and dura-dot fasteners. In cold weather this addition makes the cockpit much warmer, but the standard full tonneau cover achieves the same objective.

The mohair cover designed to fit inside the easy-up hood cover.

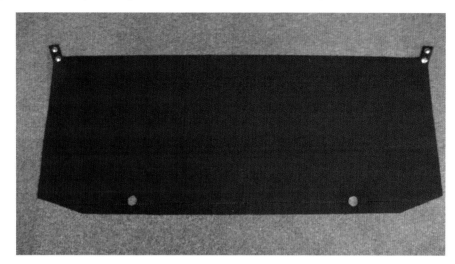

How the passenger side half tonneau cover interacts with the hood cover, the windstop, and the passenger head restraint.

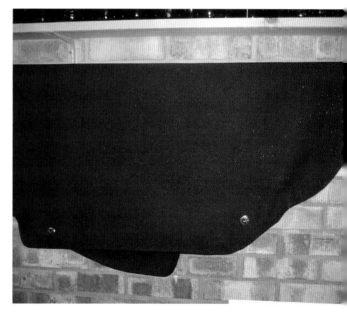

When stored, the tonneau cover hangs from two hooks, with a metal tube between. To store the sidescreen bag, use a wide coat-hanger zipped into the bag, and hung from a hook. Add a piece of brown paper between these items and the wall to prevent the transfer of dust.

Without a hood cover, when stowed, the easy-up hood will flap at both sides, as the B-post section of the hood is unsecured unless it is doubled over and tucked under the hood frame. Quite recently the factory has put this right by adding one Tenax stud each side, on to the wooden part of the frame. The Tenax fastener at the base of the B-post section of the hood attaches to this, so now there is no more flapping. This is a good and simple modification, and it can easily be retrofitted if your Morgan doesn't have the Tenax studs in the hood frame.

The current factory arrangement for the easy-up hood, where a Tenax stud is added to the frame on each side, which locates the hood and prevents it flapping about.

The hood now secured. A much better solution when the hood cover is not in use, and this feature may be retrofitted to earlier cars with the easy-up hood.

The passenger side tonneau cover, and the first design of perspex windstop. Between the windstop and hood cover is the piece of mohair that seals off the area behind the seats. This package eradicates most of the winter draughts.

FURTHER USEFUL ACCESSORIES

THE RADIO-FITTING KIT

The radio-fitting kit comprises the aerial, which is fitted to the side of the bulkhead panel, and a pair of speakers. A radio/CD can also be specified on a new-build, although some owners prefer to fit a unit of their choice after build. It's certainly worth having the aerial and speakers fitted at the build stage, although these can also be retrofitted. The speaker positions may be already cut out, and the wiring may be present in the loom, but this will not always be the case.

THE FOOT LOCKER

Foot lockers are available from Librands, to fit in the passenger footwell. This is a stainless-steel, lockable storage box with a sloping cork-based facing, which functions as a footrest. They are made in two widths, and the footwell must be measured carefully to ensure correct fitting. More recently, a foot locker has become available at the Morgan factory shop.

HARDTOPS

Hardtops are quite unusual on Morgans. A slave hardtop is used at the factory as a buck to fit the screen at the right angle. Realistically a hardtop must be hand finished to fit each Morgan, because the sidescreen position is crucial in getting the fit right. Hardtops appeared on the Morgan Motor Co. options list for a while, but at the time of writing are no longer offered on a new-build. Hardtops were standard equipment on the Le Mans '62 cars in 2002, along with a studded hood, and very occasionally still appear on Morgans for sale in the Classifieds. They were also available on the lightweight V6 Roadsters.

Don't expect a secondhand hardtop to fit another Morgan. The only way to be certain is to test fit before you buy. At the time of writing, Wolf Performance are considering the challenges of producing hardtops for the modern traditional Morgan, but there are few other options at this time, and fitting the sidescreens on to a hardtop remains a difficult obstacle to overcome on a hand-built car.

MORGAN BADGES

The subculture of Morgan badges really deserves a separate book. The range of Morgan-related badges is huge, and goes way back in time. Almost every Morgan event on the international stage, and every Morgan anniversary, has been commemorated with a badge. Most are high quality items, but some will deteriorate when used on a Morgan and exposed to the British climate. Note also that there are some very inferior quality reproductions from overseas, which appear occasionally on-line, so be very careful about what you buy on-line.

Standard chromed tube badge bars are available for Morgans with or without bumpers from a variety of sources. They are not all the same diameter, and so will need the right size badge-bar fittings, although a bracket may be sleeved on to a thinner diameter bar using rubber hose as a spacer. There is also a range of discreet flat-bar badge bars that fit over the finisher along the bottom edge of the grille. Some collectors fit badges to the luggage rack, which offers additional space for the keen collector.

There is an alternative DIY solution, by obtaining a stainless-steel number-plate backing plate. When curved slightly, this will fit behind the front number-

A stainless-steel number-plate backing plate, with additional end pieces for two extra badges. Being stainless steel, with a curved edge, makes it rigid and strong.

The completed badge bar from the front.

The finished article when fitted to a Morgan. The benefit of the stainless plate is that where certain badges have different stem length, or different spacing between the fasteners, or need spacing backwards to align, this may be accommodated by drilling the stainless plate in the appropriate places.

plate box, on Morgans with over-riders or without full bumpers. If the stainless plate is turned around so that the curved edge is inside the number-plate box, then the flat surface is available at the back, on to which the badges can be fixed. The plate may be drilled in the appropriate places to fit a selection of badges, which stand above the number plate box, but with the fixings hidden behind it. Up to five badges can be fitted.

With the badges mounted in this way, care must be taken that the fasteners don't come into contact with the lower part of the cowl. If they do,

it can and will rub the paintwork, and so it may be necessary to space out the plate slightly, or insert a rubber buffer between the badge fasteners and the cowl.

One badge in particular, the Morgan Centenary badge, has not fared well when fitted and exposed to the weather. My own Centenary badge has become badly pitted and has lost some of its paint, and even the fixing studs have started to corrode away. This is not typical of Morgan badges, but is disappointing when it happens. This badge is now in retirement on my bench after a light restoration.

CHAPTER SEVEN

THE ENGINE BAY

You might think there would be little scope for improvement in the engine bay of the modern traditional Morgan, but there are several things that can be tackled by a competent DIY mechanic.

CHANGES AND IMPROVEMENTS TO THE BONNETS

THE BONNET FASTENERS

The first thing to note is that the front bonnet fasteners have moved forwards over the years. The latest migration of the front fasteners was when the inner wings (or valances) were modified in 2013 to fit around the 3.7-litre V6 Cyclone engine. At the same time the valances were changed from stainless steel – they had been stainless steel from 1997 – to pre-formed aluminium, and were also fitted to the 4/4 and Plus 4. To fit the new valances and provide clearance, the front bonnet fasteners were moved well forward, providing an external indicator as to whether a Morgan was built before or after 2013. The valances have many holes, some of which are not used on specific models.

THE UNDERBONNET PAINT

The paint finish under the bonnets does vary. At the time of writing it seems to be to a glossy top-coat standard, but some earlier cars have a paint finish

The original position of the front bonnet catch.

The position adopted from 2013 across the range, after a redesign to accommodate the 3.7-litre V6 Roadster engine. The hand-built nature of the bonnet is also evident if you compare the gap along the front wing with the previous image.

which is body colour but satin finish. In some cases the underbonnet paint finish is grey.

THE BONNET SIDE LOUVRES

In 2004, when the Roadster replaced the Plus 8, the bonnet side louvres were reversed. Up to that point, the side louvres shared their orientation with the bonnet top louvres, facing to the rear and standing proud of the panel. The revised side louvres from 2004 are punched inwards, though still with the holes at the rear. This alteration may have been due to the fact that the S1 Roadster takes the intake air from behind the nearside bonnet via a large fibreglass trumpet, located immediately behind the side louvres.

This alteration to the side louvres was rolled out across the range, but there have been exceptions. Where the nearside bonnet has a protruding com-petition-style scoop, the bonnet side louvres revert to the original style, so facing the rear and stand-ing proud of the panel. The louvres on the scoop, however, are reverse-punched outwards in order to admit as much air as possible. Typically there will be eight forward-facing louvres and twelve rear-facing louvres on that side. This style was used on the Plus 4 Super Sport, the Plus 4 Baby Doll, and the ARP4.

The bonnet scoop design varied slightly across the Super Sport limited editions.

THE BONNET BUFFERS

The bonnets are cushioned where they touch the cowl and bulkhead by traditional woven bonnet tape. This tape must be kept lubricated, otherwise it will dry out and creak as the bonnets rub against it: this can be done with Vaseline, grease or beeswax. It is also important to keep this tape clean, because any grit that sticks to it can rub the paintwork under the bonnets.

If you suffer from a mysterious creak that seems to come from the base of the windscreen pillar, check the tacks that secure the tape to the bulkhead. Even the slightest movement of a tack into the body frame will generate a creak, which will be amplified through the frame. This may be eliminated by lifting the bonnet tape slightly and applying a dash of aerosol grease to the tack.

Despite the woven bonnet tape, the corners of the bonnets can rub on the cowl and the bulkhead, and it doesn't take long before the paint starts to wear away where this takes place. Triangular bonnet corners are available, made from leather or rubber,

A neoprene buffer added to the cowl hinge, and a perforated red leather buffer added to the corresponding point on the bonnet.

Close-up of the rear bonnet corner. A yellow leather patch is applied to the hinge bracket, and a black leather patch is on the bonnet.

The bulkhead lower corner. There is a neoprene pad below the end of the bonnet tape, fixed with double-sided tape, which causes no damage to the paint.

and these will slot over the corners and provide improved protection. The problem with this design is that over time, road dirt will get inside the protectors and abrade the paintwork on the inside and outside of the bonnets. So if you have these corners fitted, make sure that the insides are kept spotlessly clean.

Alternatively neoprene or leather patches can be attached to the bonnet corners using double-sided tape. They must be kept lubricated with Vaseline or grease. Sometimes the chassis movement is such that these buffers will migrate over time, and so they need regular checks. Without buffers, the paint will get worn away at the points of contact. It is therefore worth spending a bit of time and effort to prevent this happening.

Between the two bonnet fasteners on each side is a secondary circular buffer, which is bolted to a metal bracket, attached to the inner wing valance. On some Morgans this buffer will touch the inside of the bonnet, while on others it will not touch. A spacer washer can be inserted so that the buffer just makes contact with the bonnet. This will reduce flexing at the centre of the bonnets. Add a circular leather buffer to the inside of the bonnet in order to protect the paintwork, and keep it lubricated with Vaseline.

Very occasionally the front edge of the bonnets will rub along the curve of the cowl, despite there being bonnet tape between them. The best option if this happens, is to add a strip of 4mm neoprene along the inside leading edge of each bonnet, and this will provide just enough clearance to prevent contact.

BONNET STAYS

Aftermarket bonnet stays are available, which allow the home mechanic to have both bonnets raised at the same time. They usually fit into the rear bonnet catch bracket on the valance, by drilling a small hole into the bracket. More recently, Morgan Motor Co. have provided bonnet stays on new-builds, and these are clipped under each bonnet, adjacent to the hinge. This design of stay slots into pre-drilled holes. Before these were available, I made up a pair using aluminium tube, with simple fabricated ends, just for use in the garage during servicing. Being able to have both bonnets raised at the same time improves access considerably.

Take care when using bonnet stays outside, because a gust of wind may lift the bonnet just enough to dislodge the stay, which might cause damage to the front wing if it drops.

Bonnet props allow both bonnets to be raised at the same time, which is much more convenient when servicing. In 2004 the newly introduced Roadster was given inward pressed, side bonnet louvres, visible here. They were soon adopted across the range.

THE BONNET STRAP

Some Morgans are fitted from new with a leather bonnet strap, and some of these straps are lined with sheepskin. Sheepskin appears to be the least damaging lining material. On some Morgans you may find that the bonnet louvres under where the strap fits have been deleted, so removing the bonnet strap will leave a slightly odd look. Bonnet straps are a popular option, but unless the underside of the strap is kept scrupulously clean, road grime will accumulate and it will eventually mark the paint. Initially this will be just small scratches and dullness, but over time it will become worse.

The simplest solution to prevent such damage is to apply some paint protection film on the bonnets under the leather strap, and to take extra care in keeping the underside of the strap as clean as possible. The 4/4 80th Anniversary cars from 2016 have double straps fitted from the bottom, but these don't go all the way over the bonnets, and so should present less of a problem.

IMPROVING INSULATION

KEEPING THE UNDERBONNET AREA CLEAN AND COOL

To keep the underbonnet area as clean as possible, many of the unused holes can be sealed. This can be achieved by using a variety of grommets, or self-adhesive heat-resistant foil ('Reflect-a-Cool'). Grommets can also be added to any unused holes in the chassis rails. It is also a good idea to do a general check-over, to determine if any coolant hoses or wiring might chafe on the hardware under the bonnet. Where there is potential for contact, protection can be added in the form of rubber sheet or similar, cut to size.

Where the exhaust passes close to heat-sensitive components, it is possible to add a heat barrier by using a piece of aluminium cut and folded to fit, with heat-resistant weave or reflective foil added to it. Any sheet aluminium barrier must be properly attached using nuts and bolts or screws, and this can usually be achieved without drilling additional holes.

On the 3.0-litre Roadster, the offside (right side) exhaust manifold passes very close to both the alternator and the brake master cylinder on right-hand-drive cars. A small insulating shield can be made up to fit between the alternator and exhaust manifold, using an existing manifold stud with an extra nut added, to secure it into place. A second layer of insulation may be added to the standard heat shield fitted by Morgan Motor Co., which fits between the exhaust manifold and brake master cylinder reservoir for added protection. An aluminium tube heat shield can be made up to fit around the clutch master cylinder, which is also exposed to radiated heat from the exhaust manifold.

On the Roadster and Plus 8, reflective self-adhesive foil can be applied to the front edges of the bulkhead to reduce heat soak into the footwells. Other heat-resistant products for use in vehicles is available on-line, and could be used inside the cockpit if heat soak is an issue. Also available, and sometimes seen on the Plus 8, is a bonnet catch extender, which holds the rear edges of the bonnets slightly open, to allow the hot air to escape.

AIR FILTER AND TRUNKING ARRANGEMENTS

On the 2-litre GDI engine, the air intake tube is located in the cowl, over the radiator header tank, and the air trunking passes down the right-hand side of the engine. This is directly over the exhaust manifold and catalytic converter, and so heat soak into the air trunking is inevitable. Specialist products are available, which can be used to wrap the trunking in a reflective and insulating material, and this is well worth considering, because a cooler charge of air will provide more efficient running.

There are a number of different air filter and trunking arrangements on Morgans in this period, and it is worth looking to see where adding insulation material might be of benefit to keep the intake air as cool as possible. Modified air intake and filter systems are available from some dealers and specialists. However, beware of 'super-efficient' oiled air filters, as micro droplets of oil may disturb the mixture balance and in theory may affect the efficient running of the engine.

The Series I 3-litre V6 Roadster: the front manifold pipe passes within a few millimetres of the alternator. Here, an aluminium heat shield has been added. It is fixed using an existing manifold stud with an extra nut, and protects the alternator from direct radiated heat.

The clutch master-cylinder heat shield, made from aluminium with a reflective coating added: it simply slots over the reservoir. The steering-column universal joint is visible to the left.

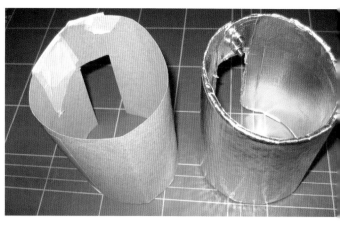

The clutch master-cylinder heat shield was created from a brown paper template with a cut-out, which allows it to slide into position very easily.

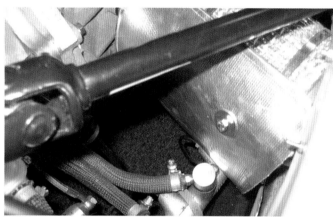

Close-up of an additional heat shield fitted between the catalytic converter and brake master cylinder on a 2-litre Plus 4 GDI. A spare threaded hole in a bracket on the 'cat' makes this a very simple modification.

A left side, inner wing valance with a large pre-formed hole, sealed using self-adhesive reflective foil, which was applied to a clean surface from both sides.

At MOT time, if your engine is at the margins of weak running on the Lamba measurement, and it has a specialist air filter, you may find that by refitting the standard filter, the Lambda measurement moves more towards normal. (I have experienced this effect in my Roadster.)

The fuel lines, both supply and return, run under the offside running board, and are very close to the exhaust for most of their length, when the exhaust is on this side. These pipes can be wrapped in a tube of silvered heat insulation weave without disturbing them, by cutting each length of insulation to fit exactly between the clips that attach the fuel lines to the chassis. The insulated tube can be secured by using self-adhesive foil insulation, or cable ties.

USEFUL IMPROVEMENTS AND PROTECTIVE MEASURES

REPLACING THE BRAKE LIGHT SWITCH

Around 2008, the classic hydraulic brake light switch was replaced with a mechanical switch at the base of the brake pedal. The original hydraulic switch, which was in common use from the sixties, is located low down on the offside (right side) chassis rail, ahead of the engine mounting, and modern versions of this switch have a reputation for failing prematurely. The switch can be replaced quite easily, and usually without having to bleed the brakes. This can be made more reliable by fitting a microswitch at the brake pedal, wired through a relay, without disturbing the original switch.

A simpler option now would be to retrofit the current Morgan Motor Co. mechanical switch on to the base of the brake pedal on the earlier cars with the hydraulic switch. Seek expert advice if you are not experienced at wiring in 12-volt accessories!

THE 3-LITRE V6 ROADSTER SUMP CLEARANCE

In the 3-litre V6 Roadster, sump ground clearance may be an issue, and this vulnerability may be a key concern if you are looking to buy your first Morgan

(see Chapter 1). The Mulfab modified sump is available to gain more clearance. Alternatively, the V6 Ford Mondeo sump will fit, but this sump uses a composite metal and rubber gasket, whereas the standard Morgan sump uses a circular section neoprene gasket, which is set into a thicker flange. V6 Mondeo sumps can be sourced on E-Bay, to have as a spare, but the specific gasket will need to be sourced from a Ford dealer.

Aluminium spacers may be added under the engine mountings. If they are made in a C shape, the bottom nut can be slackened off, and the mounting lifted from below, using a jack with an extended nut on the mounting stud. There is enough clearance at the top of the engine to gain approximately 6mm from spacing the engine mountings. Although this modification changes the alignment between the engine and propshaft very slightly, such a small change should not be a problem.

3-LITRE V6 SERIES 1 ROADSTER COIL PACK PROTECTION

The coil packs on the Series 1 Roadster are fitted high up, and at the front of the engine. They are therefore exposed to spray, and water entering through the louvres. They are also exposed to heat soak from the top coolant pipe, which is metal, and situated

A 3-litre V6 Roadster coil pack protector, fabricated by folding aluminium and adding a neoprene cover with heat-resistant foil underneath.

The coil pack protector is started by using a folded card template; this was then replicated in 1.2mm aluminium.

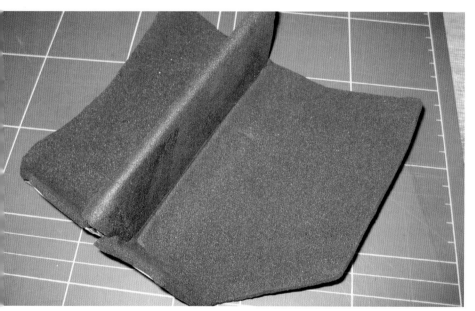

Now a layer of neoprene has been added to the underside. The next job was to add a larger high-density neoprene cover over the top, before sealing round the edges with self-adhesive reflective foil (Reflect-a-Cool).

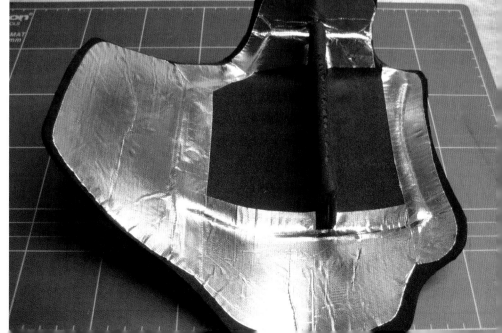

The finished coil-pack protector from below, showing the detail of construction. This slots over the coil pack with the ridge fitting between the two banks of three HT leads.

The neoprene upper surface of the coil-pack protector.

The Roadster 3-litre V6 coil pack, showing the additional insulation inserted around the top coolant hose to act as a heat barrier.

A pair of Mulfab modified V6 sumps. On the left, the lowest section of the casting has been removed. On the right, the new section has been welded into place. Many Roadster owners have taken this option to gain a few extra millimetres of clearance.

An engine-mounting spacer, made up from two layers of 2mm aluminium. Made in a C shape, it can be slotted into place by loosening and lifting the mounting, without removing it. Another 2mm layer was subsequently added, resulting in a gain in ground clearance of about 6mm.

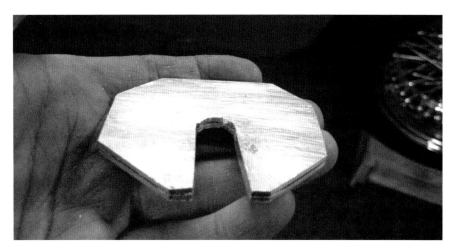

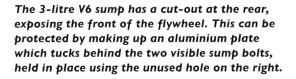

The 3-litre V6 sump has a cut-out at the rear, exposing the front of the flywheel. This can be protected by making up an aluminium plate which tucks behind the two visible sump bolts, held in place using the unused hole on the right.

The cover fixed into place, using the oversized nut and bolt, lower right.

very close to the coil packs. A length of heat barrier material can be cut to size and slotted between the top metal coolant pipe and the coil packs.

A weather shield for the coil pack can be fabricated from folded aluminium, starting with a cardboard template. This can be lined with heat barrier, and covered with neoprene. This shield will slot between the two rows of three coil packs, and will hold firm without any additional fixing. The coil pack location varies by model, and it is well worth looking at ways to keep your coil packs protected from heat sources and wet weather.

Engine Covers

The Ford Duratec and GDI engines both have spark plugs fitted deep in recesses along the top of the cylinder head, but do not have an engine cover. In wet weather, and when washing the Morgan, water will come in through the louvres. Some owners have discovered both water, and quite bad corrosion of the plugs in the recessed plug holes, even though there are rubber seals on the plug caps which should prevent this. At the time of writing, there is no off-the-shelf solution. Some owners have managed to modify the appropriate Ford saloon engine cover.

A simple engine cover can be made up using 1.5mm aluminium sheet: this has been tested over time, and has worked very well. The 2-litre Duratec engine has a convenient top coolant pipe that runs along the top left side of the engine, and the engine cover can be attached to this, via two U bolts that fit under the pipe. This leaves an exposed opening at the front of the engine, which can be sealed off with a shaped piece of aluminium, attached to the front of the cylinder head, using two existing long studs. Over several thousand miles of testing, this arrangement has not caused any problems with overheating, and has kept the plugs and the top of the engine dry.

The 2-litre GDI engine is not quite so easy to deal with, because both the engine oil dipstick and oil filler cap are within the area that needs to be protected. This means that the aluminium cover plate must have two cut-outs, unless it is made to be 'quick release'. Fixing arrangements are different on the 2-litre GDI. There are two very convenient slots on top of the inlet manifold, and two spare threaded holes can be used on the offside of the engine, if two vertical support brackets are made up, and the engine lifting eye is removed from one of them. (*See* photographs.)

A 2-litre Duratec engine cover, attached by two U bolts
around the metal coolant pipe.

The Duratec engine cover fitted around the water pipe with two U bolts, some penny washers, and some shaped plastic tubes used as spacers.

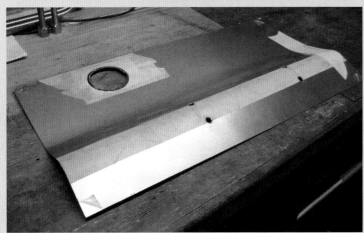

Early stages of construction of the Duratec engine cover, with the aluminium panel on the bench. The curve was achieved over a large-diameter jack handle. The cut-out for the oil filler cap was initially drilled out smaller to check the alignment, and finished off using a round-edged file.

The 2-litre GDI cover from the offside. Two support brackets were hand formed, and use two threaded holes in the block. The oil filler cap hole and dipstick hole are edged with a C-section neoprene finisher. The proximity of the exhaust to the inlet ducting is clear.

(continued overleaf)

(continued from previous page)

The GDI cover from the near side. Two supports are riveted on to the cover on this side, and these fit into the plastic slots pre-formed on the inlet manifold.

A 2-litre Plus 4 GDI showing the Reflect-a-Cool insulation on the air-intake ducting, aluminium engine cover, and modified heater-box seal. The current factory bonnet stays are clipped in position along the side of the bonnet hinge.

USEFUL REPLACEMENTS AND MODIFICATIONS

THE HEATER BOX

The original heater box to bonnet seal was a simple neoprene hollow panel seal at the beginning of this era. Originally it was shaped to fit each bonnet, and then later modified to become a single lipped seal which passed under the centre hinge. By 2012 this had become a thicker, closed-cell sponge seal, which can be quite roughly cut and is unattractive to look at. One option is to locate a suitable replacement on-line.

Alternatively, 3mm neoprene can be added to each side of the seal. It can be finished off with a neoprene or leather top, all fixed with contact adhesive. Should you decide to replace this seal, then use closed-cell neoprene, otherwise hot air from the engine bay will seep through the seal into the heater box. Sealing around the centre hinge is difficult because the hinge flanges on the bonnets move in an arc when the

bonnets are opened. To resolve this, some owners have added two more lengths of seal each side of the hinge on top of the heater box, which is how the seals were designed at the start of this period.

The heater-box air chamber has a number of short drain tubes, up to six in some cases. In heavy rain where the heater box collects a lot of water, these drains will deposit the overflow on to the top of the bulkhead, and on some Morgans this is the location of the engine ECU, inside a metal box. To improve this situation, it is simple enough to obtain some plastic tube of the right diameter, fit it over the heater-box drain tubes, and so channel any overflow away from the bulkhead and down into the bellhousing area.

If the engine ECU is in a box on the bulkhead, then check that the weather sealing is up to the mark. Current Morgans have a very well designed and sealed electrics box, but older cars are not so well equipped, and may need the addition of some neoprene seal to keep the rain out.

The 2005 heater box, with four drain tubes. Two are visible with clear plastic tubes added. Note the earlier specification lipped panel seal along the top edge of the heater box. At this time, the main fusebox was fitted through the bulkhead and is visible here.

An improved heater-box seal using closed-cell neoprene sides and a leather top. Neoprene and leather buffers are just visible on the bonnet, at top right.

THE RADIATOR

The radiator was a conventional metal unit until sometime around 2006/7, at which point a radiator with plastic tanks was adopted, and fitted slightly lower inside the cowl. In some cases, the plastic has not survived as well over time as the metal radiators have done, and these may leak around the coolant hose attachments. In the longer term, they may also leak at the seal between the plastic tanks and the metal matrix.

Aftermarket aluminium radiators are available from dealers and specialist suppliers, so if you need a replacement radiator it is worth shopping around for the best quality and the best price. Fitting a replacement radiator is apparently not too difficult, and can usually be done without removing the cowl. Very cold weather will cause metal to contract, and occasion-

ally a small leak may develop in the engine bay, where a coolant hose fits over a metal coolant pipe. Over winter, therefore, it is a good idea to occasionally check the hose clips for tightness, and also to check underneath the front of your Morgan for any damp patches.

THE HORNS

The 4-cylinder Morgans now come with a single horn under the front panel, but have the wiring in place for a pair of horns. Two horns are clearly better than one, so you may wish to source and add a second horn, or a matched pair of new horns. Should you remove the grille to do the job, then this presents an opportunity to tidy up the inside of the cowl. The grille is fixed in place by two fasteners on the bottom edge. When these are removed, the grille will slide down, and out.

The grille slides upwards into the curved channel at the top of the cowl, and is secured at the bottom with two fasteners. Care is needed, as the grille may chip the paint on the bottom edge of the cowl. Here, two neoprene side panels and a carbon-fibre lower trim panel have been added.

It locates into a channel around the top of the cowl, and great care is needed when refitting, because it is very easy to chip the paint on the bottom corners of the cowl. You may find that the two holes in the lower panel have been opened up so that the grille can be fitted squarely.

THE STEERING COLUMN

The steering column has two universal joints, and passes through the inner wing valance, protected by a fabricated metal box which is screwed on to the valance under the wing. There are two things to consider about this box. The first is that there is no grommet or seal on the forward-facing edge where

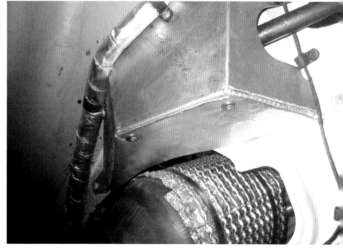

The 2016 inner wing box, which covers the steering-column universal joint. Heat-resistant weave has been riveted to the underside of the box. The box is secured with crosshead screws, and is simple to remove. The extreme closeness of the exhaust at this point is clear.

A leather grommet has been applied to seal the front of the box. The silver tube to the left is a brake reaction bar.

A 2005 Roadster inner wing box, with a neoprene front seal and top seal added.

A 2012 Duratec engine, with a simple aluminium heat shield added between the exhaust manifold and the brake master cylinder. It is attached to a blanking plate fixed to the inner wing valance, which covers a sizeable hole.

the steering column emerges towards the steering rack. This means that road dirt and spray may pass through. To remedy this, all that is needed is to add a neoprene or leather gasket to the front of the box, around the steering column.

The second consideration is where the exhaust passes just beneath the forward universal joint.

Exposure to high temperatures over a long period of time has the potential to dry out the grease and cause the universal joint to develop wear. This can be addressed by adding reflective heat-resistant weave between the exhaust and steering column. It can be attached to the underside of the box, or fitted inside it, or in both positions.

CHAPTER EIGHT

TRADITIONAL MORGAN SUSPENSION

THE FRONT SUSPENSION

Over the years – and there have been many years – much has been written in books and magazines about Morgan front suspension. It was way back in 1909 when H.F.S. Morgan decided to use the 'sliding stub axle' front suspension. It isn't sliding pillar, as most have called it in the past, but this description is commonly accepted, and regularly used, even by Morgan Motor Co. A sliding pillar arrangement is where the pin - the 'kingpin', or swivel pin – is rigidly fixed to the stub axle, and the whole assembly moves up and down, and steers, within the chassis attachment points.

KINGPIN TECHNOLOGY

Kingpins first appeared on the ends of solid beam axles, and over time were fixed into a cast C-shaped bracket at the ends of the beam. The stub axle then pivoted on the kingpin for steering, but at that time the beam axle would probably be hung on either a single transverse leaf spring, or a pair of conventional leaf springs, and so the kingpin wasn't used for suspension movement. The Model T Ford is a classic example of this early technology.

As kingpin technology evolved, the kingpin usually became attached between upper and lower wishbones, which took care of suspension movement, but the stub axle had no vertical movement on the kingpin, which remained solely responsible for steering movement.

On Morgan cars, the kingpins are long, solid, stainless-steel pins and are 2.5cm (1in) in diameter. Before 2001 the kingpins were mild steel. They attach top and bottom to the ends of the front crosshead frame,

and do not move. At the top mounting, the fastener is a robust tall bolt, sometimes called a 'lube bolt' because many of these have a grease nipple in the top, and are drilled down their length to allow greasing of the upper part of the kingpin and bush.

For a time, during the Devol bush period, some cars were built without a grease nipple in this position, and the earlier cars in this period used the one-shot oiler. In this case, the tube that resembles a brake pipe and carries the engine oil was fastened into the top of the lube bolt. The oiling was applied by using a foot pedal, and it was recommended to do this with the engine cold, when the oil would be thicker.

At the bottom mounting, the kingpin has a threaded stud that is bolted through a lozenge-shaped lower plate, the camber plate, which is fastened to the lower crosshead tube bracket using two nuts and bolts. Initially the bottom fastener was not adjustable unless the camber plate was changed, but after modification, this is now where the camber can be adjusted, using a nyloc nut.

From this point on, the kingpins have a rounded top to accommodate the adjustable camber; previously, the top of the kingpin had been flat. The main spring is mounted on to each kingpin, and inside the spring at the top is a steel cover tube and rubber tube bump stop, then the stub axle, and the rebound spring.

As already noted, up to 2001/2 Morgans were fitted with a one-shot oiler, which, when activated with the engine running, fed engine oil via metal tubes into the tops of the kingpins via the lube bolts. This process was very messy, as the oil would seep from the bottom of the kingpins and cover everything.

At the time the one-shot oiler was discontinued, so around 2001, Morgan experimented with Devol nylon bushes and stainless-steel kingpins, replacing the conventional bronze bushes and mild steel kingpins. This experiment lasted until around 2006, when they returned to bronze bushes, but retained the stainless-steel kingpins.

FRONT SUSPENSION ASSEMBLY

STUB AXLES AND DEVOL BUSHES

My 2005 Roadster was originally a Devol-equipped car, but the owner who bought it from the dealer demonstrator stock was very unhappy with the bump steer. There is an exchange of correspondence in the file between this owner and the factory, the outcome of which was that the stub axles were replaced, at a not insignificant cost, with the later revised stub axles. The benefit was that these also came with bronze bushes, and eliminated the bump steer.

The Devol cars can be converted using their original stub axles, but need oversize bronze bushes to fit these stub axles. The Devol bushes are known to swell over time, and cause stiff steering. They can also be difficult to remove. However, the science of using a nylon-type bush is sound, and a few enterprising and knowledgeable owners have experimented further with a material called Vesconite, which has proved to be long lasting and effective in use.

The stub axle begins life as a long metal tube, within which are two interference-fit bronze bushes. These bushes must be reamed (opened up) so that they are an exact fit over the kingpin. The reamer is a precision engineering cutting tool, and nowadays reamers are adjustable over a small range from the base measurement. On to the long metal tube is welded the stub axle, which carries the wheel bearings and front hub. To this is attached a heavy duty bracket, which is drilled and tapped to take the brake caliper.

When fitted, the whole assembly turns on the kingpin to provide steering, and moves up and down the kingpin to provide the front suspension compli-

A display Morgan at Cheltenham in 2009. Note the black main spring and the red rebound spring. The silver dust tube is under the main spring. The crosshead tubes are black, and the track rod is silver. Note the 'lube bolt' and grease nipple at the top of the spring.

A newly rebuilt offside front suspension assembly, with blue Mulfab steering bearing. The lower grease nipple is visible, as is the lower damper mounting pin with threaded end. The two threaded holes are to attach the brake caliper.

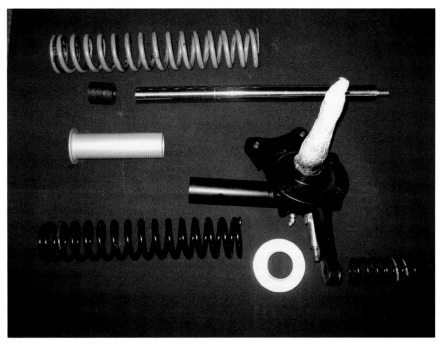

Front suspension components: from the top, original Plus 8 main spring; rubber bump stop and hard chrome kingpin (with a flat top); dust cover; stub axle; replacement Rutherford main spring; steering bearing; rebound spring. The camera flash has reflected back from the blue bearing.

ance. The main spring is above the stub axle, and does most of the work. The main spring rate has been varied over the years, and is an area to consider if you wish to modify the front suspension. Below the stub axle is a small rebound spring, which limits downward movement of the stub axle under rebound conditions.

The degree of castor (the supermarket trolley effect) is determined by the angle of the front crosshead, viewed from the side. The lower tube must be slightly ahead of the upper tube to generate the self-centring force, and is measured in degrees. At the beginning of this era, 1997, the camber angle (the angle of lean of the front wheels when viewed from the front) was still fixed, although camber could be adjusted by replacing the bottom camber plates on the lower crosshead tube. Around 2011, the factory fitted an adjustable – by nyloc nut and screw – lower camber plate, which is still in use at the time of writing.

Also around 2006, in the same period that the Devol bushes were discontinued, the stub axles were redesigned to reduce bump steer by making the track rods more level in the static position.

TRACK RODS AND STEERING DAMPER BLADES

Conventional track rods emerge from each end of a steering rack, with a spherical bearing on each end; in the classic world, the inner joints are usually adjustable for wear. But the rack on the Morgan, which eventually replaced the steering box, is very different. These track rods attach to the centre of the steering rack, and so are much longer than conventional track rods. Ideally, the track rods should be close to horizontal when static. The changes to the stub axles achieved this improvement.

For the first eight years of the modern traditional era, the front suspension continued with the long-established steering damper blades. The purpose of the steering damper blades is to separate the stub axle from the main spring. Without the bronze bearing surface between the main spring and the stub axle, suspension compression has the effect of twisting the spring and affecting the steering feel, and may cause a shimmy at speed.

But the bearing surfaces must also be held in place, and prevented from transmitting the rotational force from the compressing spring. To achieve this, the bearing is held in place by a piece of flat spring steel, located into a slot on the edge of the chassis. This is an in-and-out sliding fit, because the spring steel retainer must also flex up and down, to allow for suspension movement. The slots on the chassis are adjustable by using slotted shims each end, to close the wear gap with the spring steel. Poor adjustment of the steering dampers may cause shimmy at the steering wheel, and the chassis slots must be kept greased.

STEERING BEARINGS

Several years ago, a steering bearing kit was developed by Peter Mulberry, known as 'Mulfab'. These steering bearings are large roller bearings inside an aluminium cover, and this bearing fits under the main spring and on top of the stub axle. It replaces the steering damper blade arrangement, because now the compression twist of the main spring is absorbed by this bearing. Furthermore, it makes the steering feel much lighter.

If these bearings are fitted with the original main springs, there will be a slight increase in ride height

On the left is the current Morgan factory steering bearing. On the right is the Mulfab steering bearing. The black cover is a hard rubber. The blue cover is aluminium.

– but shorter main springs, and alternative rebound springs, plus main springs of different rates, are also available. If you choose to go down this route, you should seek advice, and then take a view on your best way forwards. Each Morgan will respond differently to modifications, so there may be an element of trial and error after fitting, to get things as you like them. If possible, always try a modified car before committing to spend money to change – but be aware that modified cars are rarely available for test, so this is not always possible.

Around 2009/10, the Morgan Motor Co. adopted their own steering bearings, and dispensed with steering damper blades. The factory bearings are slightly smaller than the Mulfab bearings, and have a hard rubber cover. My experience of these bearings on my 2012 Morgan demonstrated that the Mulfab bearings do still provide a lighter steering feel, so when I replaced the kingpins on that car, I also replaced the factory bearings with Mulfab bearings; however, I retained the original main springs, to gain a little ride height.

DAMPERS

The current factory dampers are manufactured by Spax, and give a well damped ride. AVO adjustable dampers are a very popular modification, and can be adjusted on the car. When setting AVOs, always start from the hardest setting and wind back, because at the softest setting it can be very hard to detect the clicks. Adjustment can be done by lying at the side of the Morgan – there is no need to jack the car up, but you will need a good grip, and small hands. My personal preference is eight clicks down from the hardest setting, although enthusiasts will always quote the number of clicks up from the softest setting. There are generally twelve or thirteen clicks in the adjustment range. Alternative dampers are available from Koni, Bilstein and very probably other manufacturers, and opinions do vary widely as to which offer the best ride solution.

It is not a simple task when you decide to fit different or adjustable dampers. This is very much a trial and error process, and following recommendations from other owners and specialists. What suits

From the bottom of the kingpin and crosshead, a bracing tube runs to the chassis. This is the nearside, as it was fitted in 2005. Directly above is the plate into which the steering damper blade was fitted. On this car the damper blades have been replaced with steering bearings.

The same view as the previous image on a 2016 car. The simplified fixing to the chassis should reduce damage if the front suspension is displaced backwards in a collision.

one owner may not suit another, and so you should prepare for some disappointments along the way, while hoping for the best!

FRONT SUSPENSION PRACTICALITIES

KINGPIN REPLACEMENT

Although the Morgan Motor Co. continue to use stainless-steel kingpins at the time of writing, the general view is that hard chrome kingpins are longer lasting. I have completed two kingpin replacements since 2008, and both times I have used hard chrome kingpins with spiral grooved bushes. The grooving allows for better penetration of the grease.

A competent home mechanic can certainly do a kingpin change, but this job must not be underestimated. Removal of the components is a straightforward nut-and-bolt strip-down, involving removing the brake caliper and disc, the damper and track rod end, and also the steering damper blade if

fitted. The two short bolts on the bottom camber plate must be replaced with long threaded studs, the lube bolt is removed, and then the kingpin can be wound down, thereby releasing the main spring compression.

FITTING NEW BUSHES

Always treat compressed springs with absolute respect. When on the bench and stripped down, wear will be evident on both the kingpin and bushes, but especially on the bottom bush. The tough part of this job is extracting the old bushes, and pressing in the new bushes. Access to a hydraulic press will make this much easier, but the press will need sufficient height to take the stub axle and the press tool. The bushes can be drifted out, but they will put up a fight! They can be refitted using a long threaded stud with some heavy duty washers or large sockets. With the new components on the bench, new bushes are a perfect fit over the kingpin.

The engineering problem is that at the time of manufacture, when the stub axle is welded to the long tube, the tube is distorted by this process. So when the bushes are pressed into the tube, they are nipped and put slightly out of alignment. Ideally the tube should be line-bored by a specialist machine shop after manufacture, and then in theory, the bushes could be pressed into place and the kingpin would slide into a perfect fit. Back in the real world, reaming out the bushes requires an adjustable reamer with a range of adjustment from a 2.5cm (1in) base.

THE RUTHERFORD MODIFIED SUSPENSION

The hard chrome kingpin and spring modification with AVO dampers is also known as the 'Rutherford modified suspension'. Earlier Morgans from this era, after the one-shot oiler period, may have only one grease nipple on each kingpin, but later cars have another nipple at the top of the kingpin in the lube bolt. Where a top nipple is fitted, the kingpin is drilled down the centre for a few centimetres, then side-drilled into this, with a small gallery around the kingpin. This is a very fine drilling, and some owners prefer to use heavy oil in the top nipple on each side.

The lower bush does most of the work, and should be greased regularly (every few hundred miles), taking care to keep grease away from the inside of the brake disc. If you have steering damper blades, it may be necessary to lift the bronze bearing with a screwdriver, so that grease can penetrate into the joint.

The rebound spring, and the bottom inch of the kingpin, is exposed to road grime. Many owners have devised rebound spring gaiters made from leather, rubber or mohair. Anything that keeps dirt away from the exposed bottom part of the kingpin should extend its life, because the exposed grease will quickly become grinding paste. Rebound spring gaiters can be simply wrapped around the spring, and secured with Velcro or cable ties.

The offside damper blade components: (from left to right) the blade; aluminium drop link; thrust plate. The drop link was added to provide clearance for the caliper when disc brakes were adopted.

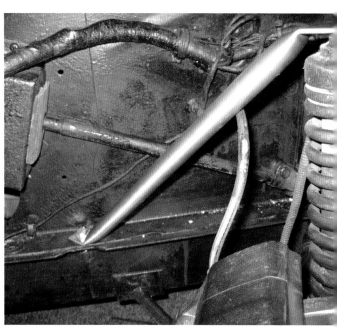

A close-up of the bracket into which the damper blade slides. Note that the two angled shims have enlarged holes: this is so they can be set up to just touch the blade, to take out any slack caused by wear.

The silver diagonally aligned tube is a brake (torque) reaction bar, which is fitted under the top lube bolt (top right), and bolted to the chassis. This is a cost-effective way to firm up the front suspension.

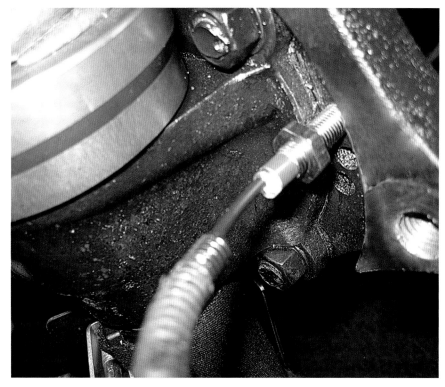

Earlier cars had a speedometer sensor on the gearbox output shaft. This was later changed to the offside front hub, where extra bolts were fitted to provide the regular pulses needed to generate a signal. This component is very delicate, and this replacement is being fitted after a breakage.

A leather rebound spring gaiter. Leather must be waterproofed when used for this purpose. It is hand-made from a soft leather offcut, with a narrow strip of Velcro hand-stitched to the edge.

MODIFICATIONS TO THE FRONT SUSPENSION

The simplest modification to the front suspension is to add brake reaction bars. These tubular bars fit between the top of the kingpin under the lube bolt, and the flat section of the chassis to the rear of the crosshead. Brake reaction bars provide a diagonal brace, which holds the crosshead more rigid under heavy braking.

Other, more comprehensive modifications are available, including Suspension Supplies Ltd (formerly Suplex) upgraded front suspension, plus a selection of brake disc and caliper upgrades from various specialists. This is all about doing plenty of research, personal choice, and how much you are prepared to spend! Power steering is currently available as standard on the 3.7-litre Roadster, and as an option on the Plus 4. It is also available as an aftermarket add-on from some specialists.

THE REAR SUSPENSION

By comparison, the rear suspension is a simple and conventional design. Earlier cars from this era will have six-leaf rear springs. These were later redesigned into four-leaf rear springs in order to soften

A mohair gaiter fitted over the leather gaiter – though mohair can be used successfully without a leather inner gaiter. Both are secured with Velcro fasteners, and can be removed easily for inspection. Also note the nyloc nut for camber adjustment, under the bottom cross-tube, introduced around 2011.

the ride. Around 2006 the rear axle was relocated slightly further to the rear, by 19mm (0.75in), to better align with the curvature of the rear wings. A kit is available from Mulfab to relocate the earlier axles, which also lowers the rear by a few mm. At the same time, the axle U bolts were strengthened by increasing them from 9mm ($^{3}/_{8}$in) diameter to 13mm ($^{1}/_{2}$in). There was a short period at the start of the four-leaf period when the springs suffered premature sagging, but this was resolved by 2012.

REPLACING LEAF SPRINGS

Should you need to replace leaf springs, then you may choose to change from six leaves to four, and specialist recommendation is to consider using the four-seater springs. These will transform the ride, and it is a step well worth considering. You might also fit the strengthened U bolts.

Changing the leaf springs is not especially difficult, but can be very strenuous, and you may need a second pair of hands. To do this job, the seats must be removed to gain access to the front leaf-spring mountings, and the spare wheel to get to the rear shackles – and even then, access is quite restricted. Good access is necessary underneath to get to the suspension U bolts, as the outer pair are shielded by the chassis and the inner pair of U bolts – so the whole job is one of working around the obstacles.

If fitting new leaf springs, then it is worth lubricating the leaves well and wrapping them in Denso tape, which will help to keep the springs protected from dirt and moisture, and will also keep their lubrication intact. Interleaving was once standard practice between the leaves, and the purpose of this was to reduce friction. Over time the practice of fitting interleaving disappeared. However, modern technology has caught up, and a synthetic self-adhesive interleaving is now available. These can only be applied with the spring removed from the car and fully dismantled, but when replacing leaf springs, this may be considered.

UPGRADES TO THE REAR SUSPENSION

Aside from replacing the rear dampers with adjustable units, upgrades to the rear suspension are few, and can be very expensive. Suspension Supplies Ltd (formerly Suplex) can supply a five link upgrade, and a rear disc conversion is available, although some enthusiasts question whether this is really necessary for road use in such a light car.

Damper options are the same as for the front suspension, and the rear dampers are quite easy to replace. At the rear it is very important to get the correct amount of travel. If the rear damper is slightly too long, it may reach the end of its travel under bump conditions, and behave like a solid rod. If this

A display Morgan at Cheltenham in 2009. Note the galvanized chassis, and the upgraded lower damper mounting on the brake backplate. 'Four-leaf' springs are fitted. This shows the elegant simplicity of a classic design from the point when the tubular rear hoop and telescopic dampers were adopted.

A Roadster in April 2017. Note the two silver anti-tramp bars, and the silver Panhard rod (optional at the time of writing), visible above the rear floor timber section. The silver electric power-steering motor is in the four o'clock position on the column. Power steering is standard on the 3.7-litre Roadster.

A rear drum with a wire-wheel hub. To remove the drum, the four small bolts should be removed. The wire wheel is a different fit to a bolt-on wheel, and so doesn't hold the drum in position. The four large, slotted set-screws should be left in place.

With the brake drum removed, to show the conventional layout that lies inside. Removing the hub will improve access when changing brake shoes, but a puller will be required to do this.

The 'six-leaf' spring fitted up to 2005/6.

happens, not only will the ride become solid with a crash, but the damper won't last very long, and it may cause damage to the mountings. Some rear dampers have integral bump stops, and this is very important to have on four-seater Morgans.

Note that in the past some Morgans suffered a failure of the bracket that secures the rear damper to the brake-drum backplate. However, this bracket has since been upgraded, and it now seems that failures are rare. A stronger bracket option is also available from New Elms Morgan in Dorset.

The 'four-leaf' spring with uprated U bolts. The U bolts were increased in diameter in 2006. Because the spring is thinner, additional threads protrude below the nuts, and the U bolt closer to the chassis has been shortened.

Some later Roadsters, from the Series 3, came from the factory with a single anti-tramp bar, and some owners have fitted a Panhard rod to better locate the rear axle. At the time of writing, the 3.7-litre Roadster is equipped with two anti-tramp bars as standard, and a Panhard rod is on the options list. At the Geneva Motor Show in

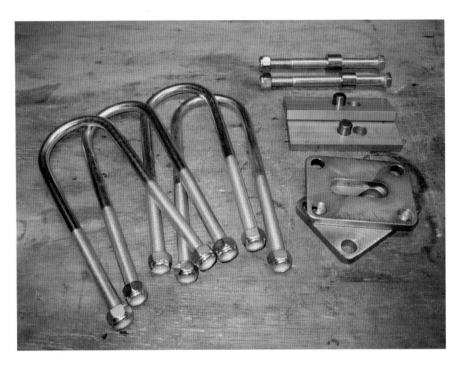

The contents of the Mulfab rear-axle spacer kit, which moves the rear axle back to align with the wheel arches. This includes U bolts, front shackle bolts with spacers, repositioning spacer blocks, and bottom plates.

2018, Morgan announced that from April 2018, the Roadster would be built with the five-link rear suspension, previously used in the limited edition ARP4. Rear disc brakes would become an aero Racing option at extra cost.

GREASING MAINTENANCE

To complete this chapter, you must also remember that the propshaft is fitted with two or three grease nipples. These, however, need only very

The rear propshaft universal joint. The rear axle is to the right, and the grease nipple is clearly visible on the joint.

The front universal joint on a 2005 Roadster: the grease nipple is just right of centre, and there is a second grease nipple on the sliding yoke, left of centre. The white plunge switch is for the handbrake warning light, and the handbrake lever pivot point is to the left of this.

light attention with a grease gun, as overdoing the greasing can pop the dust seals. The rear one on the universal joint is normally easy to access from below. At the front there may be a grease nipple on the universal joint, and there may be another on a sliding joint. Depending on the model, these may be hard to get at.

Sometimes, just making a hole at the join in the floorboards will allow access, while the angle of the nipple on the front universal joint will sometimes require the grease gun to have a special attachment so that it will reach. Close examination from below with the Morgan on a ramp, or securely lifted, will reveal how many there are, and where they are located.

CHAPTER NINE

THE TOOL TRAY

The standard Morgan tool tray is black plastic, but tool trays can be made using plywood or aluminium. Whichever method you choose, a bespoke tool tray isn't an easy job, but is well worth all the effort when it results in so much more usable storage space under the rear cover.

THE STANDARD MORGAN TOOL TRAY

The traditional two-seater Morgan has a vacuum-formed black plastic tool tray under the horizontal plywood panel behind the seats. The upper surface is finished with a black soft touch coating. The Sport models did not ordinarily leave the factory with this tray, and so owners of Sport models should expect to find no tray under the plywood cover. The factory tool tray is shallow,

and has a limited number of shaped recesses, which doesn't take full advantage of the available, but quite limited space.

Unfortunately, although the dimensions of the body frame are consistent to within a millimetre or two, the rear damper mountings, the fuel tank and the tank accessories have all evolved since 1997. This means that there is no commercially available replacement tool tray, because one size certainly won't fit all. The 2005 standard tray and the 2012 standard tray were different, and there may well be other variations.

To remove the standard tool tray, first tip both seats forward, or slide both seats forward if they are non-tilting. Next, lift the carpet, which is retained with durable-dot fasteners in the corners. This will reveal the plywood cover, which will generally have two flat plywood, elliptical swivel retainers at the

On the left is the 2005 factory tool tray – from the top: first aid kit (not provided for UK market); rectangular recess; centrelock nut spanner; circular recess, jack and handle; wheel-nut hammer; wheel-brace; second circular recess. On the right is the 2012 tray, with fewer recesses.

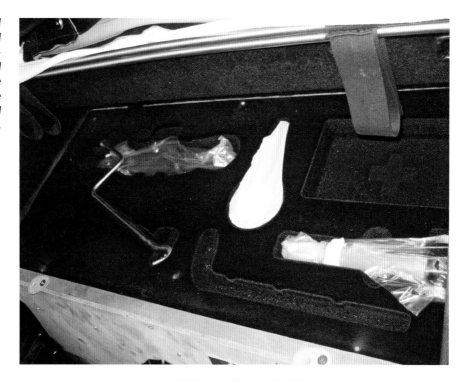

The 2012 tool tray with jack and handle, wheel-nut spanner, and hammer. From the factory, all three items came wrapped as shown.

front edge: these can be rotated out of the way. There is usually a small, clear plastic lifting tab to assist in lifting the front edge of the cover, which allows you to slide it forwards and upwards, after the seatbelt webbings are moved sideways out of the way.

The tool tray is usually fixed into place with four small crosshead wood screws. After emptying the tray of the contents, remove the screws, and it will lift at the front and slide out forwards. Over time the tool tray may become damaged, especially if the rear axle makes contact, so it should be checked periodically. With the tool tray out of the way, there is restricted access to the top of the battery, the rear damper upper mountings, the handbrake cable, and the forward part and top of the fuel tank.

The standard tool tray doesn't provide enough room for carrying additional tools or spares, so these must be carried behind or under the seats, or possibly under the bonnet on the top of the bulkhead, if a toolbox has been fitted there. A few dealers have commissioned a stainless-steel box, which locates on top of the bulkhead, to fit Morgans that have space available there.

THE PLYWOOD TOOL TRAY OPTION

The question is, how best to increase and optimize the storage space over the rear axle under the cover behind the seats? My initial thinking was to construct a new tray using plywood, to remain in keeping with the body frame construction. The advantage of a plywood tray is that ply is very easy to work with. The disadvantage is that as an amateur using wood, inevitably the outcome tends towards a square-edged, square-cornered construction.

Step one is to cut out a piece of plywood that will fit the rectangular hole in the body tub; then, after taking some measurements, cut out the centre, to better judge the available space beneath. Next, after measuring carefully, build up the box structure, and finally screw and glue it all together. It is very important to leave enough space for the rear axle casing and rear brake pipes, and to allow at least 6cm (2¼in) for upward movement from the static rear axle position.

The plywood tool tray fitted in my Roadster has survived, and is still doing the job very well after eight

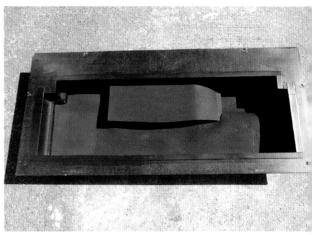

The underside of the completed plywood tool tray, painted black. The left side here (right side in the car) is slightly deeper. The circular hole provides clearance for the rear-axle breather.

The topside of the completed plywood tray, lined with neoprene sheet, which was added to prevent rattles.

There is now sufficient space for a first aid kit, tool roll, 12v compressor, spare relays, and a block of wood (silver wrapped), on which to stand the jack on soft ground.

years. It has needed only minor modifications, to provide clearance for the rear axle breather, which was contacting the bottom of the tray under hard acceleration and suspension compression. This tool tray provides sufficient space for a first aid kit, a tool roll with basic tools, a 12-volt compressor, some spare relays, and a block of wood on which to stand the standard issue scissor jack on soft ground.

It was finished in satin black, and lined with neoprene to prevent rattles. Care was taken to drill the holes to take the fixing screws in the same places as the original tray, rather than drill new holes into the body frame.

THE ALUMINIUM SHEET TOOL TRAY OPTION

This option begins with a single sheet of aluminium, and is an ambitious plan for a home metalworker. Initial thoughts were to attach a shaped aluminium sheet under a plywood cover, but it became clear that the plywood element would not be necessary for this to work. Only a limited range of aluminium sheet thickness can be worked successfully in the DIY environment. 1mm thick aluminium is easiest to work, but this is quite soft and easily dented. 1.2mm is a good compromise, but not so easy to work as 1mm, while 1.5mm is arguably the limit of amateur home working. This thickness is much harder to work, and is especially hard to curve consistently.

After taking careful measurements, begin with a flat sheet of 1.2mm aluminium, which can be obtained ready cut from a number of suppliers. The required shape is essentially an inverted aerofoil section, but it is difficult to bend and curve a large piece of aluminium, and at times it will be testing! It will need perseverance to make it fit the body tub, even before the sides are added. The side pieces are simple enough to measure and cut. They can be attached either with nuts and bolts, or pop-rivets. Double-sided tape may be used in the joins as a seal.

A hole is required in the centre of the tool tray for the differential casing, which is asymmetrical. More measuring and marking up is necessary, and after drilling a pilot hole, the opening can be cut out with metal shears. Using cardboard for a pattern, a cover can then be cut out, folded, and attached to the tray. Finally the tray must be drilled for the screw fasteners, which locate into the body frame.

The aluminium sheet tool tray, in the early stages, and still with a protective film applied.

The aluminium sheet tool tray: the image is rather flattering, but shows what can be achieved starting with a single piece of aluminium. It is fixed to the body tub by two screws into the rear panel, and two more just ahead of the differential housing cover.

The completed aluminium sheet tool tray, lined with neoprene. The additional space over that provided by the plywood tray is clear, if a comparison is made with the earlier photograph. All four fixings into the body frame can just be seen.

This option results in a roomy and worthwhile tool tray – but don't underestimate the challenge!

THE ALUMINIUM SECTION TOOL TRAY OPTION

There is an alternative and easier method for creating a tool tray. Plywood remains the simplest option, but aluminium will provide much more space. But the single aluminium sheet approach is a huge challenge, and the aluminium section method is easier: it involves fabricating smaller pieces of the tray, which can then be pop-riveted together in the car, thus ensuring a good fit.

Step one is to fabricate the two side sections, starting with cardboard templates. Smaller pieces of aluminium are much easier to work, so more space can be unlocked around the upper rear damper

The aluminium section tool tray. Step one was to form the two side pieces. Note the cut-outs for the upper damper mountings, and the shaped cut-out for the differential housing.

The rear centre section. The fuel-tank sender protrudes slightly into the space and so also needs a cut-out. The opening is lined with neoprene channel, and this is the trial fit stage.

There are four protruding bolts and nuts on the inside of the frame, which interfere with the fitting of the tool tray. Making a cut-out is simpler than bending the aluminium around the nut, and it provides a positive location.

mountings. Always remember that small variations around the damper mountings and the fuel tank means that each tray must be fitted to a specific car – for example, the 2016 fuel tank is significantly different from the tank fitted in 2012. Good metal shears are really essential for this type of work, and will quite easily fine-cut a millimetre or two from the edge of a piece of aluminium. The side sections are small enough to be fabricated in a bench vice, using a mixture of timber sections and square-section aluminium, assisted by G clamps, in order to get straight and consistent creases.

Step two is to make the two centre sections, which fit at the front and rear of the differential housing. The front piece is a simple rectangle, with two light folds. The rear centre piece is more complex, as it may need a cut-out for the tank sender, depending on the year of the Morgan involved. If a cut-out is necessary, then the hole must be covered with another aluminium piece. After shaping, these pieces can be placed into the body tub, and marked, drilled and pop-riveted.

The tool-tray sides and upper damper mounting covers must be prepared using cardboard templates, before cutting out and folding the aluminium, and then test fitting, adjusting and riveting the pieces into place. A thin neoprene sheet fixed inside the tray using aerosol adhesive will reduce rattles, but it is also a good idea to wrap heavy items in either neoprene or bubblewrap. Underneath, consider fitting some neoprene pads between the tool tray and the top of the fuel tank.

Whichever method you choose, a bespoke tool tray isn't an easy job, but is well worth all the effort when it results in so much more usable storage space under the rear cover.

The test fit. Now only the differential casing cover is required, and some clearance for the brake pipes.

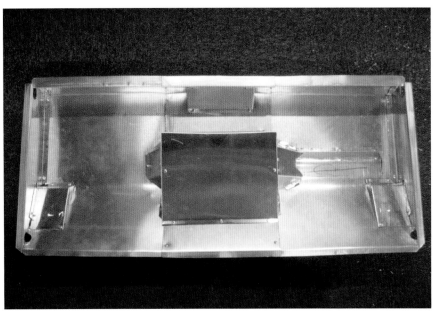

The aluminium section tool tray, almost complete. Note the upper damper mounting covers each side, the fuel sender cover (top centre), and the centre differential casing cover. The extended cover to the right is to clear the brake pipe; this was later modified to provide additional clearance for the flexible hose.

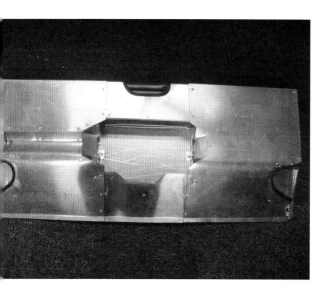

The underside of the aluminium section tool tray. The edges around the rear damper mountings are dressed back slightly using a hammer, and edged with neoprene channel, as is the edge around the fuel tank sender. All the seams are pop-riveted through double-sided tape to provide a good seal.

The tool tray was completed with a neoprene lining to prevent rattles. This tray locates well, around the four protruding bolts in the body tub. The original flat plywood cover fits over the top. The front swivel fasteners must be spaced slightly using washers, to accommodate the thicker tool tray.

The completed aluminium section tray, with tools added. There is just room to fit the scissor jack behind the differential housing cover. Everything else fits with room to spare. Compare this to the original factory tool tray earlier in this chapter.

Working with Sheet Metal

Working metal is not something that can be learned from a book! 'Hands on' is the only way, and begin small. Safety is paramount, and metal fragments tend to be sharp, and can also fly through the air. Take sensible precautions when sawing and drilling metal: use eye protectors, and wear gloves. When using power tools to sand, file and drill, or when applying spray paint, it is also a good idea to wear a breathing mask. When working in the garage, always make sure that any vehicle parked inside is protected from flying metal fragments.

It has been said that Peter Morgan once told a journalist that Morgans were built to a point where the customer could finish off each car to their own specification. For some enthusiasts, this is the whole point of owning a Morgan, and can be a huge attraction to the marque. Autojumbles are still a very valuable source of a variety of metal offcuts, but the internet now also allows easy access to sheet metal cut to size, as required for each job. With a selection of aluminium sheet

from 1mm to 2mm thickness, and a good selection of metal shears, almost anything is possible. With practice, and with a good sized bench vice, plus G clamps, and stout timber and metal formers, it gets easier to create sharp creases in aluminium, and eventually you will feel confident enough to progress into curving sheets.

Once aluminium is mastered, then you can move on to stainless steel. Stainless is much harder to work with, and needs top quality drills, especially if you don't have a vertical bench drill, but it can be worked reasonably well in small panels, and looks very good when finished.

To summarize, it is all about having a lot of practice, and being prepared to throw failures away and start again. Have good metal snips and good quality drills, and you will need a decent-sized bench vice! A supply of thin but stiff cardboard is essential for 'cardboard-aided design'. Always begin with a pencil, a straight-edge, and a cardboard template!

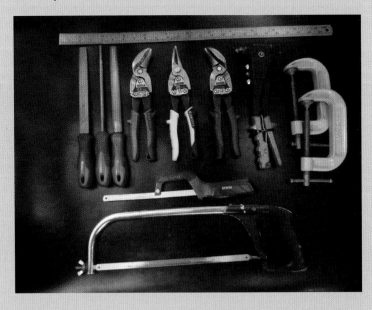

A basic metalworking toolkit. From the top: a steel rule, three files (one is half round), three pairs of metal snips (straight, and curved each way), pop riveter, G clamps and two hacksaws.

Bending sheet aluminium in a bench vice. A pair of steel or aluminium L sections, or box sections, would also work well. The G clamps ensure that the fold is consistent, but the key to doing this is to measure accurately, and to position the piece accurately in the vice.

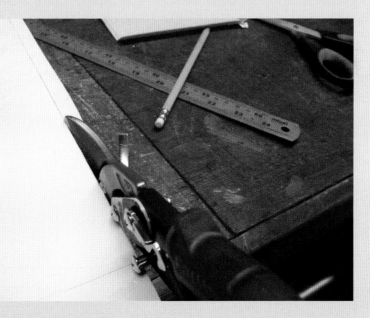

Cutting aluminium in a straight line. First measure, then scribe, and then cut with confidence and a decent pair of metal shears.

CHAPTER TEN

THE UNDERTRAY AND FRONT VALANCE

Many modern cars have a complex form of undertray, which in most cases completely encloses the engine bay. Morgans do not, and this is primarily because the design comes from an era before undertrays had been considered. To add some perspective to this, in late 1977 the MGB engine bay was given a refresh by British Leyland. As part of this upgrade, the radiator was moved forward. The space between the engine and the repositioned radiator was then fitted with an 'acoustic shield' (as described in the parts list), attached to brackets on the front 'chassis legs'. This enhancement was made from a stiff fibreboard panel, and was shaped at the rear to provide space for the crankshaft pulley. This was my first real encounter with an undertray. In the world of MG concours, this item was sometimes replaced with a fabricated aluminium plate to the same design.

The benefit of an undertray or shield is that it prevents road debris coming into contact with the crankshaft pulley and drive belt, and it also reduces the amount of dirt and water spray that can penetrate into the engine bay.

The front end of the traditional Morgan is a very open design, and the crankshaft pulley and drive belt is exposed on all the traditional cars, as is the lower section of the radiator. Around 2006, the radiator was lowered in the chassis, when the plastic tank version was introduced, and so from that point on, more of the lower part of the radiator becomes

A brace of Plus 4 Super Sports up the hill at Shelsley Walsh, showing the standard factory front valance for that model. Note that these models don't have an intake cut-out below the grille.

The first ARP4 at the Silverstone Classic in July 2015. It has a very attractive valance, and a centre intake below the grille. Note the wide gap between the cowl and headlamp nacelles, due to the wide alloy wheels, and the wider front frame (from 2010).

A Wolf Performance bespoke full-width valance, available to order with an optional centre intake in a variety of shapes. A narrow version is available for cars with over-riders. ADRIAN SLADE

exposed on these later cars. Some limited edition, performance-based Morgans were fitted with a front valance as a standard fit. This is much simpler to do when neither bumper nor over-riders are fitted at the front.

There are three locations to consider when thinking about adapting and fitting an undertray to a traditional Morgan: between the engine and the crosshead, from the crosshead to the front of the Morgan, and as a front valance.

LOCATION ONE: BETWEEN THE ENGINE AND CROSSHEAD

The first area for attention lies between the front of the engine and the rear of the front frame, or crosshead. The Plus 8 and 4-cylinder cars have quite limited space in this area, but the V6-engined cars have a significantly larger space due to their shorter engine, which also appears to be mounted slightly further back in the chassis. The exposed area stretches from the crankshaft pulley to the rear of the lower crosstube.

When considering fitting an aluminium tray here, remember that the lower crosstube is the designated jacking point at the front – refer to the owners' handbook. This means that jack access to the crosstube should be maintained. I will cover this particular point in more detail in the next chapter. When designing an undertray for this section, stiff cardboard is essential to get the template the right size and shape. The chassis rails converge quite sharply ahead of the engine mountings, so the aluminium section will be a trapezoid shape.

A completed aluminium Plus 4 undertray, with a curved front edge to add strength. It is asymmetric because the Plus 4 Duratec engine is offset in the engine bay.

The undertray from the previous photograph, now fitted above the chassis rails. The upward curve at the front is to allow access to the crosstube for jacking.

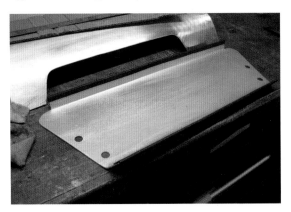

The latest design, with four holes to utilize the towing-eye fasteners, and with the front and rear edges turned up to add stiffness. Edged with U-channel neoprene, this undertray fits underneath the chassis rails, using neoprene pads to avoid metal-to-metal contact.

View of the fitted undertray from behind the front wheel. The towing eye is wrapped in yellow tape to aid visibility in the dark, should this be needed.

The undertray can be either slotted in over the flat sections of the chassis, and then slid forwards, or fixed below them. Aluminium that is less than 1.5mm thickness may need reinforcement on the edges to reduce flexing; alternatively, bending the edges front and back into an L shape will create extra stiffness. The towing-eye fixing bolts, although oversized for this role, can be used to hold the undertray in place on one side, and the corresponding pre-drilled holes can be used on the opposite chassis rail. I prefer not to drill the chassis wherever possible, and have used penny washers with nuts and bolts to secure the undertray, when there was no other alternative.

My first attempt at this job was on my Roadster. First, I cut out a shape that would slot above the chassis rails and slide forwards into place. This was secured by a combination of using the existing holes in the chassis, and with penny washers at the rear, which overlapped the chassis rails and held it securely. The second time I did this job, on my 2012 Duratec-engined Morgan, I used the same method but the undertray was a different shape, because the Duratec engine is slightly offset in the engine bay. This means that the undertray is asymmetric.

My latest and most recent design for filling this space on my current Plus 4 has folded edges front and rear, and fits under the chassis rails. Because this version fits underneath, it is a very simple shape with two simple straight folds front and rear to add stiffness. This design could easily be mass produced.

LOCATION TWO: FROM THE CROSSHEAD TO THE FRONT OF THE MORGAN

Now moving forward, let's consider how to apply the undertray treatment to the space between the lower crosstube and the front of the Morgan. How easy this will be, does depend on whether or not the particular Morgan has over-riders fitted. With over-riders, there is a pair of robust brackets that are bolted to the crosshead in exactly the right position to attach a flat, rectangular aluminium undertray. It may be necessary to use spacer washers between these brackets and the undertray to provide sufficient clearance, and the undertray may need to be contoured downwards slightly at the front to clear the base of the radiator.

This undertray panel is fitted to the over-rider brackets and is forward of the lower crosstube. Three of the four fasteners are visible. Note that the front edge has been shaped downwards slightly to clear the radiator.

If the undertray touches, or comes close to the radiator, then a small neoprene buffer should be placed between the two, to cushion shocks and prevent rubbing as the chassis flexes. It would not be appropriate to provide any dimensions for this, because each Morgan will be slightly different. The over-rider brackets are handed, and are vertical in cross-section, but also have a ledge on one side, and so have a 'sideways T' profile. These brackets may be fitted to each Morgan as a pair, with the ledges facing inwards or outwards.

Where the ledge of the T faces inwards, this job is particularly simple, because these ledges are already pre-drilled in two places on each side. Where the ledges face outwards, four small bespoke aluminium brackets must be made up to secure the undertray, but the existing holes in those brackets can still be used to secure the made-up aluminium brackets. These four additional brackets can be cut and folded from sheet aluminium, of a minimum thickness of 1.5mm, starting with the usual cardboard templates.

Morgans without over-riders don't have these brackets, and so a more complex arrangement would have to be designed to fit an undertray in this position on these cars. The over-rider brackets, or full bumper brackets, could be adapted to do this job, by cutting off the forward ends. Morgans with a full front bumper have tubular, rather than angle brackets to support the bumper, which could be used as a starting point, but bespoke fitting brackets would still be necessary.

LOCATION THREE: THE FRONT VALANCE

The previous two undertray solutions perform an important function, but are not visible unless the bonnets are lifted. The front valance is not an undertray, but is very closely related, and is visible, forming part of the Morgan face. Most competition Morgans have a valance in one form or another. The standard traditional Morgan doesn't normally have one, but some limited edition Morgans with a competition style such as the Plus 4 Super Sport and the ARP4 were provided with a front valance by Morgan Motor Co. The ARP4 valance in particular is a very attractive design.

Eight years ago when I started out with Morgan, valances were not generally available, except from competition specialists. At the time of writing, a

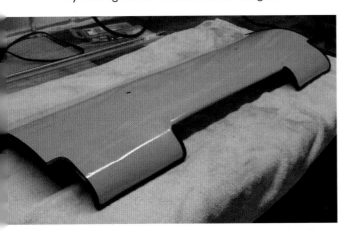

The one-off short front valance ready for fitting. It was made from 1.2mm aluminium, which, because it deforms easily, has had the lip of the aperture turned over to add stiffness. C-channel neoprene seal has been added as a finisher.

The final fitting of the short valance to the car. It attaches to the aluminium undertray pictured earlier in this chapter. The front number-plate box is still to be refitted, to finish the job.

selection of valances are available from specialist companies (for example, Wolf Performance). They vary in width to match the variable width of front wings across the traditional Morgan range, and also have the option of circular holes at each end for brake cooling. There is a choice of centre aperture shape with an option of a mesh grille, though this will be partly covered if the front number-plate box is retained on over-rider and non-over-rider Morgans.

The design of the over-rider brackets makes it difficult to design a single-piece front valance for over-rider cars, although a narrow valance is available from Wolf to fit between the brackets. So the majority of Morgans with a full valance are without over-riders or a full front bumper. However, it is possible to design a valance to fit around tubular full bumper brackets.

For a while, Morgan Motor Co. supplied a lower cowl extension that was designed as a rectangular intake, with vertical grille members to match the cowl. By the time I looked into buying one they were no longer listed and so are quite rare, but also quite distinctive. So for my 2012 Morgan I made up a short front valance that fitted up to the base of the front wings and cowl, and went part way back over the aluminium undertray between the over-rider brackets.

This was very much a learning curve. I made this up from 1.2mm aluminium, which is very easy to curve but lacks stiffness. To stiffen up the centre aperture I therefore turned the bottom edge back on itself, and added a C-section neoprene finisher. Once painted to match the bodywork this looked very good and prepared me for the bigger challenge ahead.

THE DIY CHALLENGE: FULL FRONT VALANCE

It is possible to amalgamate the undertray that fits forward of the crosshead with a front valance. To do this, fabricate a single curved piece of aluminium to fit over the area from the lower edge of the front wings and cowl, right back to the front edge of the lower crosstube, using either 1.2mm or 1.5mm aluminium sheet. This can be sourced from the internet, already cut to size.

The more recent long valance after shaping and cutting, in the initial fitting stage. It also shows the design of the over-rider brackets. (This is not the same yellow car as featured earlier in this chapter.)

The hardest part of taking up this DIY challenge is getting a progressive curve on the visible front section. With patience and a large bench vice, assisted by G clamps and stout timber, this is just about possible at home if you are able to use a round former (such as a scaffolding pole or large jack handle) to get the right shape. Once the curve is in place, the front aperture can be measured and cut out, using a hacksaw and metal snips. The outer surface will probably need filing to get a consistent outer curve, and this takes time. Several trial fits are necessary, both to get a good fit around the crosshead, and to sort out where to drill the holes for the brackets.

Once the panel is prepared, it then becomes a matter of patience, applying primer and paint, followed by lacquer, and lots of flatting down, until a

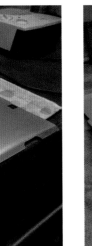

The completed long valance, drilled, and with small leather washers around the fixing holes. The rear edge has been shaped in two places to fit around the crosshead brackets. After road testing, it was necessary to add a strip of adhesive neoprene along the rear edge to stop resonance.

The painted side of the completed long valance. Only the front edge has been trimmed with a C-channel neoprene finisher. Compare this to the short valance pictured earlier in this chapter. Good quality metal snips are essential.

The standard front-end layout on over-rider cars. The front number-plate box adds more protection when fitted, but the exposure of the lower part of the radiator is obvious. Note the grille fasteners (long bolts), which I prefer to fit from the rear.

satisfactory finish is obtained. And if a home solution is a step too far, there are professional metal shapers in the Morgan world who would be able to perform this task easily!

To finish off this job, small side valances can be fabricated to fit either side of the standard over-rider brackets, and attached to them using angled brackets to give the look of a one-piece front valance. The photographs in this chapter will hopefully provide some inspiration as to what can be achieved with patience.

Sealing off the underside makes a big difference to what can get into the engine bay, and is well worth considering. The easier option is to buy a ready-made valance, and have it professionally painted and fitted.

The long valance is now fitted, using the four fasteners and bespoke brackets, and the existing holes in the over-rider brackets. Compare this to the previous photograph.

The front with the number-plate box refitted. The number-plate box isn't universally popular, and some owners have removed it and hung the number plate in this position using brackets from the grille, or have used an adhesive number plate on a front wing.

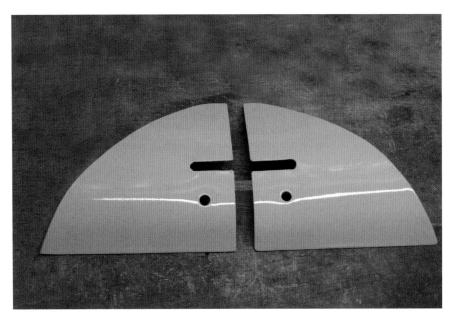

Extending the front valance to either side of the over-rider brackets can only be achieved by making a pair of end pieces. Here they are being painted. The slot is to allow the piece to slide over the ledge on the over-rider bracket, which on this Morgan faces outwards.

The end piece of the valance is attached to the over-rider bracket with a bespoke aluminium bracket. Also evident is the outward-facing ledge on the over-rider bracket. The front valance bracket is just visible (lower right), closely fitted to that bracket, and using an existing hole.

Close-up of the end piece from the front. These pieces needed some 'final adjustment' to get the position just right. The neoprene edging will prevent any metal-to-metal chafing as the wings flex.

The completed front valance. The finished article is quite subtle, and not as visible as some of the other front valances available at the time of writing.

A Front Spoiler

As noted earlier in this chapter, in 2008 only the competition specialists supplied front valances. At that time I wouldn't have contemplated using a sheet of aluminium as a DIY starting point, but I couldn't help thinking that the front of the traditional Morgan as it leaves the factory is too open to the elements. It wasn't long before I had fitted undertrays to my Roadster, but the open front aspect remained a niggle.

I wondered if a fibreglass spoiler from another car might be made to fit. I had fitted such a spoiler to my MGB some years earlier, and the BL Special Tuning spoiler did actually make a difference to the steering feel at speed. The Morgan and MGB are similar sizes at the front, and so I took the plunge and ordered an MGB spoiler. When it arrived I then faced the problem as to how I might cut this fibreglass monstrosity without making a mistake and having to scrap it. More head scratching followed, until I had a flash of inspiration.

It was suddenly obvious: papier mâché. I spent the next few days laying up newspaper and glue, without really knowing if this would work or not. I left it for a week to dry and harden, and then came the moment of truth: it separated from the spoiler and was an exact replica. It exceeded my expectations, and any slips with the scissors now could be reset with more newspaper and glue. So next, I painstakingly started cutting the papier mâché spoiler until it fitted the front of the Morgan. Before starting this I had removed both

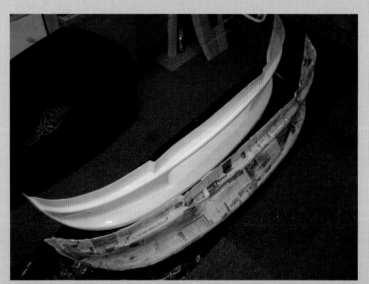

The papier mâché spoiler mould and fibreglass MGB spoiler after separation.

The fibreglass spoiler cut and shaped, and ready for fitting.

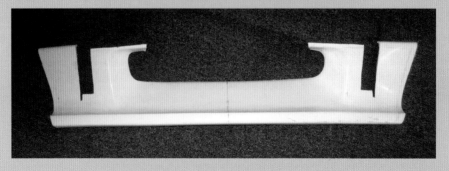

the over-riders and the number-plate box. Once I was happy with the fit, I stuck the template to the real spoiler and started cutting and shaping, and it wasn't long before I had a workable spoiler.

How to fit it was much more of a challenge. I try not to drill extra holes, and so I concluded that the best way to fasten the ends was by angled brackets on to the over-rider brackets, using penny washers. Around the cowl it was more difficult, but there are two nuts and bolts on each side of the lower front panel, and I decided to use these existing fasteners, and make up some special brackets. However, the angle of these brackets was not straightforward, and it took several attempts before I got this right.

The spoiler was then painted Corsa Red, and edged with C-section neoprene finisher. It has a centre airscoop, which puts the airflow into the bottom tank on the radiator, and the lower intake lip exactly matches the undertray between the over-rider brackets. It has now been fitted for over eight years, and has worked really well. Obviously this looks rather unusual, when most Morgan valances curve the other way! At the time of writing, I am wondering whether to replace it with a full length traditional front valance, as I have fitted to my Plus 4. This will be another challenge to consider in the coming year.

CLOCKWISE FROM TOP LEFT:
The spoiler is fitted without drilling extra holes. Upper left is a bracket that uses an existing fastener on the front lower panel. In the right foreground, penny washers locate a right-angled bracket on to the over-rider bracket.

This style of lower front spoiler won't be to everyone's taste, but it does do the job!

From the normal viewing position the spoiler is very discreet; from a distance it can look slightly odd because of the reverse curve and angled ends.

CHAPTER ELEVEN

SERVICING AND MAINTENANCE

Many enthusiasts who come to Morgans later on in life have a long history of hands-on involvement with classic cars. In fact, having developed such life skills is one of the factors that drives some enthusiasts towards the Morgan brand, especially the traditional Morgans. For any owner wishing to undertake home servicing or home maintenance, the right size garage, and the right tools are essential.

Safety first in the garage is essential:
• Always use eye protection when using power tools
• Always use protective gloves when metalworking
• Use a breathing mask when sanding and filing
• Beware of hot surfaces when using a blowlamp, soldering iron, or reaching into a hot engine bay
• Always beware of rotating drive belts and pulleys when the engine is running
• When any vehicle is lifted off the ground using a jack, don't venture underneath it, however tempting, until the wheels touching the ground have been chocked, and additional means of support, such as axle stands or stout timber blocks, are in place

HAND TOOLS AND EQUIPMENT

Most enthusiasts will have collected tools over a lifetime, and will have an array of socket sets, open-ended and ring spanners, and a selection of screwdrivers, pliers and saws. A good variable speed hand drill is an essential item, with a wide selection of top quality drill bits. A vertical bench drill is even more useful on occasions, but not quite so common in a typical enthusiast's garage. A soldering iron is also a good tool to have for occasional use.

Morgans are simple cars, and most of the fasteners will be imperial AF, with an occasional Whitworth fastener. Engine and gearbox fasteners on more modern Ford engines will have metric fasteners. Morgans do have a number of Allen-headed fasteners, and so an Allen key set will also be necessary at some point. Replacement fasteners are sometimes needed when doing a job, and there are several companies that can provide nuts and bolts in a variety of sizes and materials. Avoid using stainless-steel fasteners on stressed applications without taking professional advice; some stainless steel can be brittle, and is not suitable for suspension components.

TROLLEY JACKS AND JACKING BEAMS

A trolley jack is also an essential, and this must be a lowline jack, so that it will fit under the Morgan. Two trolley jacks are even better for added flexibility. Note that some modern trolley jacks have a front roller between the frames, however this is not as stable an arrangement as having two wheels outside the frames. The scissor jack, which comes as standard with most Morgans, is only meant to be used for changing a wheel at the side of the road. It is good practice to carry a small block of wood on which to stand this jack, should you be unlucky enough to find some soft ground. Similarly, a hydraulic bottle jack certainly has some limited uses, but it is not the best option for home servicing.

The first thing to become familiar with, is where to place the trolley jack. The designated jacking points are covered in the Morgan Motor Co. owners' handbook, but because we are dealing with a separate

A full front jacking beam. The raised U channels at each end locate on the crosshead lower tube, and the three raised blocks spread the load. The angled piece locates on the towing eye. The three rectangular blocks were later thinned down to clear the undertray.

A rear jacking beam, as first designed and still in use. The long rubber section is raised above the base timber on a thin length of wood. The two smaller blocks with holes in the top locate on two 'lift-the-dot' studs that are fixed into the floorboards.

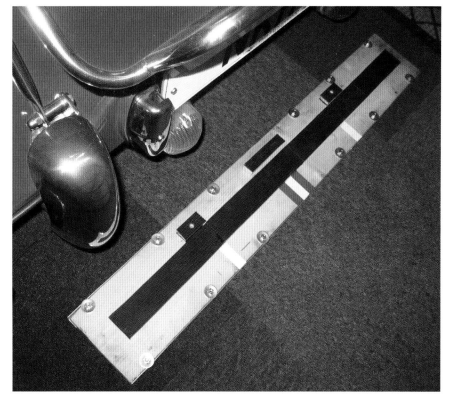

In use, and the three bolts line up with the white tape markers. The trolley jack is aluminium and low, and may be sourced from the internet.

chassis, the normal rules don't apply. Whenever possible, avoid lifting just one side or just one corner of a Morgan: doing this puts a lot of strain on the chassis, so it is much better to lift either the front, or the rear, from a central point.

At the front, the jack should be placed under the centre of the front crosshead lower tube. This tube is stronger than it looks. At the rear, the nominated jacking area is under the rearmost chassis cross-member, to which the rear valance is attached on Morgans without full bumpers. This rear crossmember is double skinned and so is strong enough to support the weight. However, when a dealer uses a four-pad lift, they will generally use the triangular sections under the bulkhead outer corners, and at the rear, the double-skinned crossmember ahead of the rear wheels, which carries the spring mounts.

You may consider using this method to lift the front or rear using a trolley jack on either side, but it is not recommended by Morgan Motor Co. as the nominated method. Never jack up a Morgan anywhere else along the chassis rails, because it may cause damage by bending the lower chassis flange.

For routine home servicing and maintenance, it is worth making up your own jacking beams, because there are no Morgan-specific jacking beams cur-

rently available. Either timber or metal is suitable for this job. I chose timber, starting with what was basically a length of floorboard, and I chose this method because wood is easier to modify – I'm now on version number three at the front. The timber used for the front beam fits from kingpin to kingpin under the lower crosshead tube. When using a trolley jack in the centre, the lifting beam will sag at the ends. I reinforced the timber with aluminium L-profile edges, which are bolted into place. But even with this strengthening added, the timber still flexes slightly when taking the weight of the Morgan.

This jacking beam locates on to the crosshead tube at each end using an aluminium U channel, fixed on wooden spacer blocks to get the right height. The beam also has a raised wooden section in the centre where it touches the crosshead, so that the load is spread along the full length. Underneath the beam in the centre I have added a rubber pad to prevent the jack slipping, and I have marked the centre of the crosshead tube with electrical tape. This arrangement has worked very well, even though the crosshead tube on my Morgan is partially masked by the undertrays on either side of it.

The front jacking beam isn't suitable to use under the rear crossmember, which is the designated jacking

Hammers or Mallets

Hammers are a very important Morgan service tool. If your Morgan has centrelock wire wheels, or the optional centrelock alloys on some Plus 8s and the 4/4 80th Anniversary cars, then it will probably have a wheel-nut hammer, and this is usually made by Thor. Thor hammers have been in business for a very long time, and they are beautifully made. The ones that come with new Morgans have a head which I understand is antimonial lead. The more impressive-looking Thor hammers have one end cap made of copper, and the other end is a thick hide roll. This model is known as the 'Copper-hide'. I like Thor hammers so much that I bought one long before I needed one for centrelock wheels.

The Thor range is extensive, and also includes 'dead-blow' hammers with nylon faces in addition to other metal-faced options. The most popular-sized Thor for centrelocks is the 'No. 2', which is 1,070g (2.36lb). This is the size I have had in my toolbox for many years, and it has had a lot of use. More recently I have added a 'No. 1', which is 710g (1.56lb), and a 'No. 3', which is 1,600g (3.53lb). I find that the 'No. 3' is at my limit of preference; it is quite heavy and unwieldy to swing, but obviously does the job when it connects.

My Morgan dealer favours a Thor dead-blow hammer for centrelocks, and a year or so ago I also added one of these to my toolbox. This type of hammer comes in a bewildering array of sizes between 453g (1lb) and 1,925g (4.25lb). I settled on catalogue number 1616, which is 1,250g (2.75lb), since this weight falls between the weights of the 'No. 2' and 'No. 3' Copper-hide Thor.

From the left, the Copper-hide Thor 'No. 3', dead-blow '1616', Copper-hide 'No. 2' and 'No. 1'. The 'No. 2' has seen a great deal of use, and I recently replaced the hide cap, which had gone beyond saving.

A stand-alone wooden block in use on its side. These blocks can also be used turned through 90 degrees (clockwise). Small wheel-stops were added so that the Morgan can't roll off when in the highest position. They provide a stable platform and good access.

point, so I have made up a flat, full-width jacking beam for this location, with a raised section which locates on to the rear crossmember. The construction is the same as for the front beam, with aluminium L-profile edges, and I have covered the contact area with rubber to avoid damage. It fits just in front of the rear valance fixing bolts, which provide a good reference point, especially the bolt in the centre. I also have a mark on the beam as a reference point for the centre point.

Note that when the Morgan is jacked up at the extreme rear, the flexing in the chassis means that the doors won't open or close cleanly; it is therefore better to keep them shut properly when jacking at the rear.

Invest in a good quality, low-line trolley jack, because it will last for years and be invaluable. I made up four large wooden blocks a few years ago from some offcuts which I had available. I can use these blocks either on their sides or standing up, and they provide safe access under the Morgan when used. I do also have a pit in the garage but only use it very occasionally, as it has filled up with non-car-related storage items.

CENTRELOCK NUTS

There are three types of centrelock nut: earless, which are sometimes known as 'continental', the two-eared spinner, and the three-eared spinner.

Earless nuts: Although earless nuts have eight sides, they are sometimes referred to as 'hex' nuts. The standard spanner for these nuts is a large ring spanner in flat steel, which doesn't usually fit the nut particularly well, and can damage its corners. Dealers and specialists can supply alternative wheel-nut spanners, and a brass open socket is available from MWS, which when fitted over the earless nut, provides two ears for hammer action. Some Morgan dealers can supply a large, purpose-made socket, which will take a long breaker bar. This tool can remove an earless centrelock effortlessly, but it is heavy and unwieldy to carry when touring, and so is better kept at home.

The two-eared spinner: This is probably the most popular type of nut, and the most common centrelock nut, and has been fitted to many sports cars over the years. Normally these are removed using a soft-faced hammer. A wooden adapter is available from specialists, which fits over the spinner, and absorbs the hammer blows without damage to the ears.

The three-eared spinner: These were often used on more exotic cars, but are available to fit Morgans. It provides an additional place to hit with

the soft-faced hammer, but otherwise it is similar to the two-eared variety.

Aftermarket spinners are available from specialists such as MWS, with or without the Morgan script engraved on the centre. In my more recent experience, I have found that black or painted wire wheels tend to grab the centre nut, and this can make it much harder to loosen off. There was a period when

An earless or continental spinner on a stainless-steel Roadster wire wheel, with the Morgan script picked out in red. Some colours show better than others on the spinners.

The three-eared spinner on a stainless-steel 4/4 wire wheel, with the Morgan script picked out in yellow. Note the wheel-balance weight, top left. There is no space on the 4/4 wire wheel to fit adhesive weights to the outside of the rim.

A two-eared spinner on a black 4/4 wire wheel. Where the black wheels are fitted, the balance weights are painted black on the outside of the rims. STEVE HARRIS

A continental spinner tool in the form of a socket with a breaker bar. I obtained this tool from Ledgerwoods (the Morgan dealer in Lincolnshire) in 2008. It is a very effective tool.

I had earless spinners on black wire wheels, and I found that these were impossible to loosen without first carefully heating up the nut with a blowlamp. In contrast, when stainless-steel wire wheels are fitted, I have never struggled to loosen the nuts.

Where the wheels are wider, as on the Roadster and Plus 8, extra care is necessary when swinging the hammer on to a recessed centre nut. A misplaced swing may damage the rim. A very light coating of grease or Coppaslip around the outside of the wire-wheel centre, where the spinner locates, will help to prevent the coating grabbing the centre nut.

THE FRONT BRAKES

The Lockheed calipers fitted up to 2008 go back a very long way, and are easily identified by their rough-cast iron surface and electroplated finish, which is a pale gold colour when new. The brake pads are retained by conventional split pins with spring H clips.

These were replaced with Caparo (AP) aluminium brake calipers at the same time that the steering damper blades were replaced with steering bearings. The Caparo calipers can be identified by their smooth black finish, and orange Caparo branding on the outside faces. These calipers also have external brake pipes, which link each side of the caliper. They often come with orange plastic 'top hat' covers on the bleed nipples. The brake pads are secured by 'dumb bell' shaped pins, which are retained very simply, each by a spring H clip: these must be depressed so that the pins may be drifted out. The pads are identical for both types, and are the same pads as were used for the Austin Princess.

Caparo calipers do not fit on to earlier Morgans with steering damper blades. The disc pad set on the current Caparo price list is shown as HF201 (MBS1734). The reference number on the actual pad is LB2LGNO11A E344. The reference on the original Lockheed pads was MXD 1142FF 23648 4U. The

The Lockheed caliper with split-pin retainers, with EBC Greenstuff pads, and on this Roadster, EBC brake discs. The upper lube bolt and grease nipple are very clear.

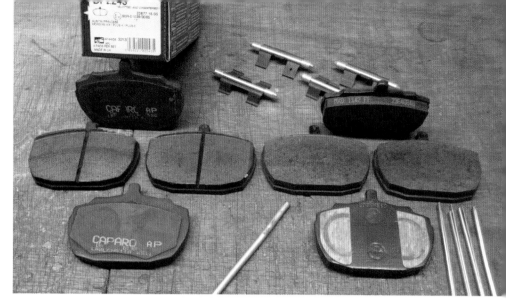

The EBC brake-pad box. Below is a set of Caparo brake pads. To the right of these are Lockheed brake pads. To the right of the pads are split pins from the Lockheed calipers. Upper right are the 'dumb bell' retaining pins and spring clips from the Caparo calipers.

The later Caparo caliper. It is very different in appearance to the earlier Lockheed caliper, and will not fit earlier Morgans with steering damper blades. Note the upper lube bolt and grease nipple, and the brake reaction bar to the right.

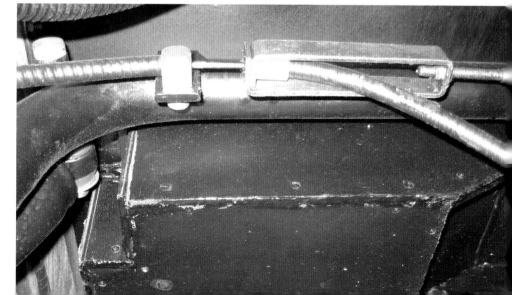

The handbrake adjustment, a conventional long-threaded stud with two locknuts. The circular mark in the tool tray to the left is where the rear axle breather has made contact. I later cut out a small hole here to improve clearance.

Caparo pad retaining pin is listed as LB08H9035AP, and the spring and pin kit is listed as HCK215. The spring clips are available from Rimmer Bros under part number QP2740. Finally, the flexible brake hose is listed thus: LH/RH MEL50932LP(LH5955)-MBH0330.

The Caparo calipers have a slight misalignment between the disc and brake pads, and a thin ridge of unworn pad material will build up over time on the outside edge of the pad, as it wears. It is important that the pads are inspected at service time, and when necessary, the ridge is filed away, always using a mask to avoid inhaling the dust. Lockheed calipers are much better in this respect, but there may still be a very slight wear ridge in the same position, and so the owner should be aware of this, and inspect the pads occasionally.

Aftermarket EBC Greenstuff pads are DP2243. I have used these pads for eight years on my Roadster, and they have been very good in use, with minimal brake dust and good braking performance.

GREASING

A good quality grease gun is an essential servicing tool. Both my grease guns were inherited when my relatives moved on to cars without grease nipples, and that was many years ago. But my peculiar taste in cars has meant that all my cars have always needed greasing regularly. One grease gun is unbranded, and the other is a Wanner, made in Switzerland, and a highly regarded brand in grease-gun circles. However, the truth is that my unbranded gun is the equal of the Wanner. Both date back to the late 1960s and both are basically still as new. I have a flexible nozzle attachment, and a small box of flexible joints to reach those unreachable nipples.

Greasing is an art, and those new to it often struggle, but the secret is very simple. The grease-gun nozzle must be fitted and held absolutely square on to the nipple, with a degree of pressure; the slightest angle, or release of pressure, will cause grease to come out of the side, rather than go into the nipple. When the grease is going where it should, there is a particular feel to the grease-gun handle of smooth

resistance, which is very similar to the feel of compressing a telescopic damper.

Opinions vary as to how often the front suspension should be greased, and what grease should be used. In terms of how often, then I would consider a 1,600km (1,000 mile) period as an absolute maximum, and I prefer to grease up every few hundred miles. Some owners will take their grease gun with them when touring, and small grease guns are available for this purpose. Certainly, if a touring holiday is likely to exceed 1,600km (1,000 miles), this is a good idea. An alternative is to find a village garage that is off the beaten track, and which will be likely to have greasing equipment to hand.

With regard to the type of grease, I tend to favour moly grease, but conventional grease, or the denser red and tacky grease will also do the job. Some owners use heavy oil in the upper kingpin nipple on each side, but earlier Morgans in this period from 1997 do not have an upper grease nipple, and some cars may still have the one-shot oiler system in place.

A remote greasing kit is available, and this places the grease nipples on to the inner wings, with a flexible connection to the kingpins. This modification makes the actual job of greasing much easier and cleaner, but the area between the kingpins and inner surface of the brake discs must be inspected from time to time to ensure that no grease can come into contact with the discs. The propshaft has two or three grease nipples, depending on the model, but these need only very occasional attention. A flexible nozzle may be needed to gain access to the front of the propshaft from below, and it may be necessary to open up an access hole in the floorboards in order to reach the front grease nipples, again depending on the model.

When filling a grease gun, first pull back on the spring pressure and secure the chain. Unscrew the grease reservoir, and then slowly release the spring pressure until the grease residue is level with the rim of the reservoir. Insert the reservoir into the tub of grease over the hole in the plastic shield, and then press down gently while at the same time pulling back on the chain, until the reservoir is full. Secure the chain, and screw the reservoir back on to the grease gun. Release the chain and open the bleed valve until all the air is expelled.

Some Wanner guns have two bleed nipples, and the one above the grease reservoir is the one for bleeding the air. If the handle is not firm at this point, there may be more air to bleed from the reservoir. When pumped, there should now be a continuous bead of grease from the nozzle with a firm pressure at the handle.

THE REAR BRAKES

The rear brakes are conventional drums with a conventional handbrake, and are Ford Transit in origin. The only exception to this is the limited edition ARP4, which has rear discs, and a handbrake that acts on the discs. Morgans with centrelock wire wheels have two sets of fasteners that are visible on the brake drum face: there are four slotted flat set screws, which should be left alone, and four small conventional bolt heads, which secure the drum on to the rear hub. Centrelock wire wheels don't hold the drum in place, unlike conventional bolt-on alloy wheels, which is why they have these retaining bolts. (For images of the rear drum and rear brake shoes, see Chapter 8.)

The current Caparo price list shows the wheel cylinders as LB1LCK023AP (CW15953), the repair kit is HWK110 (LK10543), OEM/Orig Ref MBS1240, and the brake shoe retainer set is HF207. The EBC brake shoes are shown as 6380, 230 [x] 45mm.

The brake drums should be removed at service time so that the linings may be examined, and the wheel cylinders checked for leaks. Check the handbrake cable periodically, because some Morgans have suffered the outer cable splitting where it enters the brake-drum backplates. A split will allow water to get inside and rust the inner cable, which may then weaken and break. This is not common, but does occasionally happen. 3-in-1 oil can be dribbled inside the cables each side when the tool tray is removed at service time.

The brake fluid should be replaced at two-year intervals. I have completed this job many times, and the old fluid usually emerges in a very discoloured

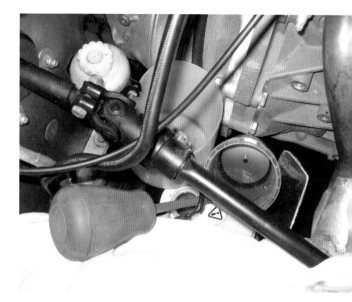

A fluid transfer tool in action, taking the old fluid out of the brake master cylinder.

Two-year-old brake fluid, which came from the rear brake nipples. When bleeding the brakes use plenty of rags, something to lay over the front wing for protection, plastic containers, ring spanners to fit the bleed nipples, a bleed tube, and a good supply of brake fluid.

state, especially from the rear. I also replace the clutch hydraulic fluid at the same time, although this has an easier time than the fluid in the brakes. To make this job easier, I have a fluid transfer tool. This is made like a chicken baster, and its purpose is to suck out most of the old fluid from the master cylinder reservoir, before replacing with new fluid. This method saves time, because the old fluid in the master cylinder doesn't then need to be pumped through the system first.

DOT4 fluid is now the preferred standard in road cars. DOT5.1 is essentially a competition fluid, and can be used but must be changed more regularly than DOT4. Both these fluids are glycol based, and have a higher boiling point than DOT3. DOT5 is silicon based and cannot be mixed with any of the other types. The pros and cons of changing to DOT5 silicon fluid have been well aired over the years in the classic car press, and the argument is outside the scope of this book, except to say that the concensus view seems to be that it should only be first used in a new, dry braking system.

THE BATTERY AND ELECTRICAL SYSTEM

On two-seater Morgans, the battery will either be mounted under the bonnet on the front bulkhead, or it will be behind the seats under the rear panel on the left side. When it is situated under the rear panel, access is via an aluminium plate behind the passenger (left-hand) seat, and also by lifting the tool tray.

The battery is held conventionally by two wing nuts on the end of long-threaded J rods, with a retaining crossbar in between. These wing nuts are prone to seizing, and so will benefit from being occasionally loosened off, and lubricated with Coppaslip or grease. A battery-charging cable will make that job much easier, and the positive cable must be fused for safety. The cables can be fed through a hole drilled through the rear panel, with the connecting plug conveniently kept in the corner behind the left-hand seat, under the carpet. The battery will last much longer if it is regularly connected to a battery conditioner.

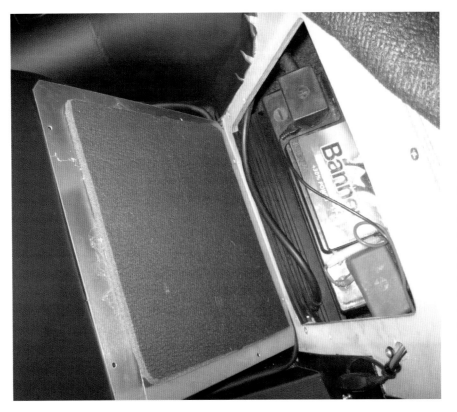

The aluminium battery access panel. Additions are the charger lead, which emerges through the rear panel, lower right. Also ahead of the battery, a strip of rubber has been added as a splashguard, and a camping mat has been cut to fill the hole and provide insulation and sealing.

The master fuse on a 2012 Duratec Plus 4. It is located in the upper right-hand corner under the dashboard. This fuse was found to be not fully located, and so was retained by cable tie.

Somewhere in the electrical system there will be a master fuse or master switch. This can be situated under the dashboard, or close to the battery, or in the electrics box on later cars. It is worth locating this item for future reference, and to make sure that if a master fuse is fitted, it doesn't vibrate from the holder. Note that isolating the battery may reset the engine ECU to the factory default settings. On the left side of the bulkhead you will also find the inertia switch. This cuts the 12-volt fuel-pump supply in the event of an accident. This switch may also be tripped by travelling over rough roads, so if the power suddenly fails, look at this switch first. It is a simple push-to-reset switch.

The relays are usually under the dashboard, either centrally mounted, or over the steering column on right-hand-drive cars. On later

Morgans, most of the electrics have migrated to a sealed metal box on the right-hand side of the bulkhead. When sourcing replacement relays you must specify diode protection, which will prevent current surges and possible damage to sensitive components, including the engine ECU.

The front indicator units will sometimes start to fill with water over time, and if not checked, will suffer quite serious corrosion of the bulb fixing area, resulting in no current passing. In the worst cases this will require a new lamp backplate, as the bulb holder may corrode beyond repair. The lens is held in place by two long machine screws which locate into rectangular brass top-hat nuts, fitted from the rear of the lamp unit. There is a soft rubber weatherseal, and the lens locates into the lamp unit with a small peg that ensures the correct alignment. This

The components of the front indicator lamp unit. Rear lamps are the same, but with different lenses. From top left: orange lens; rear of the lamp unit; front of the lamp unit; two versions of weatherseal; and screw fasteners, seals and brass top-hat retainers, which fit behind the lamp body.

lamp unit may also have a chromed plastic reflector, but sometimes they are absent. The rear lamp units are the same, except for the lenses, and the fixing screws are shorter to match these shallower rear lenses. So there are two lengths of fixing screws and two types of thread.

Some owners choose to fit clear indicator lenses with orange bulbs. These are a straight exchange fit at the front, but at the rear will require longer fixing screws, and may need the top hats changing if the thread is different. Note also that some orange bulbs have offset pins, if you choose to go down this route. Where clear rear indicator lenses are fitted, you may wish to change the sidelight/brakelight lenses to a matching shaped red lens. These are available, and are a standard fit on some Aero 8 models.

All light units should be checked routinely for the ingress of water. LED replacement light units are available, but may not conform to legal requirements in some territories.

THE EXHAUST MOUNTINGS

The exhaust mountings should be examined occasionally, as the rubber bobbins may perish over time. If you decide to replace any parts, then take a photograph before you start, because some of the components will fit either way round, and once dismantled it may not then be clear how things were fitted before. The U bolts are generally 54mm on modern Morgans, and these are available on-line in stainless steel. The rubber bobbins are standard Mini/

The Chassis Number

Morgan chassis numbers follow the conventional system as required by current legislation. The chassis plate is secured to the bulkhead, right-hand side, and may be on the upper surface of the bulkhead, or the side panel. The chassis number is also stamped into the right side chassis crossmember, just ahead of the driver's seat on right-hand-drive cars. The chassis plate is glued in place, but has four pre-drilled holes. It is therefore a huge temptation to add cosmetic screw heads into these holes!

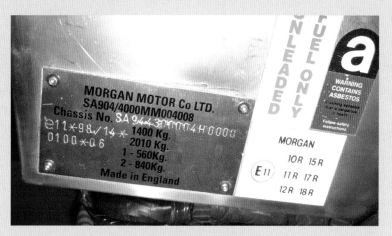

A 2005 S1 Roadster chassis plate, with the last four digits photoshopped to zero. The plate is glued in place on the upper surface of the bulkhead, and the four Allen-headed screws are cosmetic additions, secured with Araldite.

The Body Number

The body number is allocated to the body frame in the wood shop. My 2005 Roadster has body number 525, but at the time of writing, the body number is four digits. My 2012 4/4 Anniversary was body number 4133, and my 2016 Plus 4 has body number 5987. The body number is stamped into the ash frame, and is visible on a built-up car in two places. One stamp can be found under the carpet, adjacent to the tool-tray panel on the right-hand side, and the second stamp is adjacent to the spare wheel mounting plate on the left. The body number and build number bear no logical or numerical relationship to the chassis number.

With the spare wheel removed, the body number is visible to the left of the spare wheel mounting plate.

The Build Number

This is the factory control number, and follows each Morgan right through the factory from step 1, which is the build book, basket of components and a bare chassis, to the final stage of signing off for delivery. Build numbers do not necessarily pass through the factory in numerical order. At the time of writing this is a six-digit number, now in the range '101000'. This number appears in several places on the body panels, and is most visible on the inside of the bonnets near the hinge. The build number is also stamped at the rear of the front wings, and the front lower edge of the rear wings.

If a Morgan has a black Dinitrol underseal, then it will be a struggle to locate these numbers without the assistance of white spirit. More recent Morgans also have the build number stencilled on to a hood fabric tag, which is attached to the hood on the left side above the sidescreen frame. It isn't clear how long this has been standard practice. My 2005 Morgan doesn't have the build number inside the bonnets, and it doesn't appear to be stamped into the wings, although there is a thick layer of underseal, which I don't intend to disturb. So even where the build number might prove elusive, you should be able to locate the chassis number and the body number quite easily. However, this was not always the case with older Morgans!

The rear edge of the nearside (left side) front wing, looking back towards the brake drum; the build number can be seen.

The basic components of a single exhaust mounting. This U bolt has been refinished in heat-resistant silver paint, but stainless steel is a better long-term solution.

MGB parts and are freely available on line and at specialists. Some bobbins come with slightly longer studs, but this doesn't impact on fitting.

Modern Morgan exhausts are stainless steel. They fit to the catalytic converter with a spherical joint, overlapped with a stainless-steel convex clamp. This is secured with a conventional, single, round-headed coach bolt, and usually comes from new with a number of spacer washers, and a standard-sized nut. To aid future removal, it is a good idea to replace these with a single spacer washer and an elongated nut, which covers all the exposed threads. When refitted with Coppaslip, this will undo much more easily if necessary in the future.

The stainless-steel exhaust system was introduced across the range as part of the 1997 improvements.

Long stainless-steel silencers are fitted under one or both running boards, depending on the model, with a further joint ahead of the rear wheel, which is secured by the exhaust mounting at that point. Behind this is either a single section with an integral tailpipe silencer, or a two-piece section, which may have a short tailpipe silencer or a simple straight tailpipe. Side-exit exhausts are available for the traditional cars, and these emerge just ahead of the rear wheels.

A range of sports manifolds and exhaust systems are available from specialists. These are claimed to release more power, and are usually noisier than the standard system. So take advice before fitting a sports exhaust system, or you may fit a system that you then discover is too noisy!

OIL CHANGES – ENGINE OIL

All the engines used by Morgan in this period are conventional mass-produced units, and most are built by Ford Motor Co. They all have conventional sump drain plugs, oil filler caps and dipsticks, with one exception: the ARP4, which has a dry sump, and so doesn't have a dipstick. On this model, the oil level is marked inside the oil tank on the left side of the engine bay (on right-hand-drive cars).

The Rover V8 engine was designed in the days when a 20w50 oil was the norm, and I would recommend staying with this grade, as modern 20w50 oils are available and are suitable for this engine. The Ford engines are all much more modern designs, and will generally take a 5w30 or 5w40 grade. Recently I have been using Mobil Super 3000 fully synthetic oil, but other quality brands are available.

Most Ford engines now take a standard filter, which began life as the EFL600, but is also known generically as the 'Zetec' filter. At the time of writing this filter has a long part number, which any Ford dealership will be familiar with. Interestingly the Mondeo ST220 filter doesn't fit the Series 1 V6 3-litre engine. This engine will accept the Zetec filter, but I prefer to source my filters from the local Jaguar dealer, as the filter that fits the S-Type and X-Type cars will fit the Roadster engine, and is slightly larger than the Ford filter. The current Jaguar part number is XR8E 6714AC.

So all you need do for a home oil change is simply confirm which grade oil is recommended for your particular engine, and source the right filter, which can be cross referenced to other brands if necessary.

GEARBOX OIL

Some enthusiasts will be happy to subscribe to the 'filled for life' approach to gearbox oil. I prefer to change the gearbox oil occasionally; it doesn't need to be annually, and the mileage covered should be taken into consideration.

Some of the gearboxes fitted to Morgans in this period will take automatic transmission fluid (ATF), and some will take gear oil:

- The Getrag 221 gearbox fitted to the Series 1 Roadster is specified to take Esso LT71141 ATF
- The MX5 gearbox in later Duratec Morgans should take 75w90 gear oil
- The Rover R380 was originally specified to take Dexron III ATF, but this appears to have been superseded by Texaco MTF94
- The Getrag/Ford MT-82 gearbox in the 3.7-litre Roadster takes either Ford XT-11-QDC or Castrol BOT 130M oil
- The Ford MT-75 gearbox is more confusing, as this gearbox was 'filled for life'. There is an MT75 gear oil, but some owners have used 75w90 gear oil, although this option may stiffen the gearchange when the oil is cold

In all cases, before you change the gearbox oil, do some research. Remove the filler/level plug first, just in case it won't come out. The filler/level plug is in various locations, depending on the type of gearbox fitted. On the Getrag gearbox it is accessible in the right-hand footwell through an access hole in the transmission tunnel. On later Roadsters with the Ford MT-75 gearbox, it is on the left side. On the MX5 gearbox the filler/level plug is on the left side, but is accessible through the engine bay. Some gearbox plugs are a conventional shape, and some are the more traditional tapered square heads, which need a specialized spanner for best results.

Drain the old oil through the drain plug rather than pumping it out through the filler/level plug. This will ensure that any residue or sludge will be purged from the casing.

REAR AXLE OIL

Very similar principles apply to the rear axle oil as to the gearbox oil. The drain plug is normally the lowest bolt head on the rear cover. The most regular grade oil is 80w140, and this is available in semi, and fully synthetic specifications. If the Morgan has a limited slip differential (LSD), then the axle will also require a friction modifier. Some rear axle oil comes with this already added, but it can also be sourced from performance specialists such as Demon Tweeks.

To check whether you have a limited slip differential, first lift the rear of the Morgan. Next, turn one rear wheel by hand. If the opposite rear wheel rotates the same way, then you have an LSD. If it rotates the opposite way, then there is no LSD. Some rear axles do have a metal tag on the filler/level plug which indicates that an LSD is fitted. Limited slip differentials do tend to darken the oil, so expect the old oil to be darker than you might expect. Where there is insufficient friction modifier in the axle, you may experience a judder, especially when reversing, which may sound like a loose wheel. If this occurs, then adding a small quantity of friction modifier should settle things down.

I use a 2ltr plastic ice-cream container to catch the oil from the gearbox and rear axle. First, check that your gearbox capacity is no more than two litres! Filling the rear axle is best done with the tool tray removed, and using a funnel with an extension tube. Filling by this method is quite slow due to the viscosity of the oil. Morris Lubricants are used by Morgan Motor Co., and I have used their transmission oil, which is available on-line, since 2008.

THE MORGAN WHISTLE

Some, but not all Morgans, will produce a whistle when on the road. It almost sounds like air passing over the top of a bottle, and although the pitch doesn't vary too much, the volume will increase with speed. This sound comes from the headlamp surrounds, where air passes between and over the surround and the headlamp unit. Morgan do fit a short neoprene seal between the two components, but sometimes this is not enough to silence the whistle.

All it takes to banish the whistle is a length of self-adhesive neoprene strip. It doesn't need to be more than a few millimetres deep or wide. After removing the headlamp surround, the strip must be stuck either around the headlamp unit, or around the inside of the rim towards the front. When the trim ring is refitted, the neoprene strip doesn't show.

Before removing the headlamp trim, stick a small piece of masking tape on top of the headlamp nacelle, and mark the position of the small raised bump on each one. This will make it much simpler to line up the fixing screw upon refitting. An offset screwdriver makes this job easier, although removing the orange indicator lens will also improve accessibility.

ODDS AND ENDS

The wing beading must be kept lubricated, using 3-in-1 oil or similar, and this should also be used on the locks and hinges. Insert the door key part-way into the door lock, drop some oil on to the key, and it will wick into the lock. Don't overdo the oil on the hinges, or it may emerge on to the door when driving, and make a mess. The bonnet tapes must be kept lubricated using Vaseline or similar, otherwise creaks may develop. All the exposed nuts and bolts should be checked at service time, including the wing stays and wing fasteners, because these fasteners do vibrate loose on Morgans.

CHAPTER TWELVE

TOURING HOLIDAYS

Many Morgan owners use their cars as fair weather weekend cars, and this is why so many Morgans have such a low mileage as the years roll by. Other owners will use their Morgan much more regularly, and a few more hardened enthusiasts will use a Morgan as a daily driver. But nothing beats the experience of a touring holiday in a Morgan, especially when it involves driving through glorious scenery.

COPING WITH WET WEATHER

Inevitably, when doing this, at some stage you will experience wet weather. It therefore makes sense to take some sensible precautions. These precautions should be to keep things dry inside the cockpit (or tonneau), and to keep the luggage dry. Most of your luggage will be forced to travel outside on the luggage rack, unless there are just two occupants in a four-seater Morgan. How to minimize rain getting into the cockpit when the hood is in the raised position has already been discussed (see Chapter 3), but often it will be lowered or removed when the rain begins to fall.

Our road trip experiences have shown very clearly that it is good practice to carry a couple of towels when on the road touring. Our towels are black, to match the upholstery, and although they haven't had too much use, they travel tucked behind the seats in a cloth bag. They need to be handy! It's also a good idea to carry a few absorbent paper napkins, although kitchen roll will do the same job. Sometimes the rain will begin to fall at an inconvenient moment, in mid-journey. Sometimes it will only be a shower, so you can drive through it by increasing speed until the rain blows over, although this does depend on the type of road and the traffic density.

However, there may come a point when you will begin to wonder if you should stop and put the hood up. If your Morgan has sun visors, the rain will blow over the top of the screen frame, wet the visors, and build up to a point when it will drip down on to the occupants' legs. In this situation, the towels can be deployed to cover laps and thighs. This may also happen to a lesser extent with the hood in the raised position, if it has a poor seal on the top of the screen frame.

With the hood stowed, the rain will also eventually wet the head restraints, and it will swirl over the screen frame and wet the inside of the windscreen. When this happens, the paper napkins can be used to clear the inside of the screen. It's worth hanging on to clean, used napkins for this purpose, and they are also useful for dealing with spills in the garage. Slowing down for roundabouts and junctions can become quite unpleasant in rain, especially if you wear spectacles, because the eddies and swirls will eventually coat both sides of your lenses, and at this point it becomes dangerous to continue.

On the motorway at speed it is possible to press on through quite heavy rain without getting wet, but leaving the motorway, and finding a place to stop to raise the hood will soon see the occupants and the interior of the Morgan soaked, unless you practise raising the hood in advance. The easy-up hood is marginally quicker to erect than the studded hood in this situation, but not by much in terms of how wet you might get. When out alone with a half tonneau cover fitted over the passenger side, the driver may sometimes choose to drive on regardless. Be prepared for some odd looks if you choose to drive in the rain with the hood down!

The small cockpit cover in place over the soft top. Note that the two elasticated ties fit to the rear, around the luggage-rack mountings.

STORM COVERS

Three sizes of storm cover are available. A small cockpit cover from Walker St Clair came with my Roadster, and we also have two storm covers from John Taylor (Phoenix design). One is a slightly larger cockpit cover, which I recently obtained to use on my Plus 4, and the other is an extended cover which also protects the bonnet louvres.

There are alternative suppliers of storm covers, so do some research and talk to your dealer. A small cockpit cover is the most convenient for regular use, and this can be positioned over the hood, or over the cockpit with the hood lowered, or with the hood removed, as in the case of the traditional studded hood. The cockpit cover can be used even when the hood is travel-stained or dirty.

A cover is essential when parking near the coast, to protect the hood from seagull droppings and tree sap, especially if the hood material is mohair. In heavy rain the cover will prevent water ingress into the cockpit – the only problem is finding somewhere to dry it after overnight rain, although sunshine will soon dry the nylon-type fabric. The cockpit cover does also add an element of privacy, because it is not possible to look inside the Morgan with the cover fitted.

The large storm cover extends across the bonnet louvres, and the elasticated straps fit around the headlamp nacelles, the door handles, and around the rear wing corners and rear lamp tubes. We have used this cover overnight when the forecast was for heavy and persistent rain. However, I wouldn't use it if the

John Taylor's large storm cover, which also protects the bonnet louvres. Note the multiple securing straps, which fit around the headlamps, bonnet fasteners, door handles, rear wings and rear light units. The elastic straps may rub the paintwork if the car is dirty, so care is required.

Morgan were travel stained, because in windy conditions the elasticated straps will move slightly, and any dirt could form an abrasive paste, which may mark the paint. I therefore only use the large storm cover when the Morgan is clean.

If you are unfamiliar with fitting a storm cover, have a practice run or two in the garage first. In windy conditions it may be a challenge to fit, so some familiarity with the fitting process is beneficial, especially if you have an audience when trying to fit it! You may consider marking the cover by wrapping coloured pvc tape round the ends of the elasticated straps, for example green for offside, and red for nearside. This makes it immediately obvious which way round it

fits, and which side is down! Also note whether the maker's label is outside or inside when fitted.

The small storm cover will easily slot behind a seat, but the larger cover takes up more space when folded, and this needs to be allowed for when touring.

Beyond the storm cover range there are full tailored car covers, both outdoor and indoor, for use at home, and these are available from Morgan Motor Co., dealers and specialist suppliers.

THE FOOTPUMP

We always make sure we have a method of inflating the tyres at the roadside, and carry either a twin-barrel footpump or a 12-volt compressor. The footpump will fit behind the seats, and the compressor will fit either behind the seats or in a bespoke tool tray, but not in the original plastic tool tray. My concern with 12-volt compressors is that if the fuse blows in the supply socket, it then becomes much more of a problem. The loose nature of 12-volt socket fittings can occasionally blow the fuse, which makes the old-fashioned footpump a much safer option.

RELAYS

The relays are known to fail very occasionally. Spare relays must be diode-protected against any spikes in the 12-volt supply, rather than using simple standard unprotected relays. Morgan dealers, Land Rover specialists and auto electrical suppliers will have these in stock. Where the relays are situated in your Morgan varies, and it is worth tracking them down before you need to replace one, which might be in the dark. There may be four or five, and they are usually in a row. A bigger relay is there to provide the wiper delay function.

In 2005 the relays were under the dashboard, just above the steering column (on right-hand-drive Morgans); by 2012 they were under the dashboard

in a central position. Later cars have an electrics box on the right-hand side of the bulkhead under the bonnet. There will also be a master fuse, and/or a master switch, and these may be behind the rear shelf adjacent to the battery (if the battery is at the rear), or in the top right-hand corner under the dashboard, and possibly elsewhere on earlier cars, some of which had the battery on the bulkhead under the bonnet.

It is now possible to buy a portable mini jump starter/battery pack, which is a compact, state-of-the-art battery, no larger than a small book. We have one of these, but have not tested it yet as a jump starter. However, it can also be used as an external battery pack for mobile phones, sat-navs, and other similar items, and so may be worth carrying for peace of mind.

THE TOOL ROLL

It is worth carrying a basic tool roll with a small selection of tools, not with the intention of undertaking roadside repairs, but simply for some reassurance. It is good practice to include a selection of fuses, some baling wire, and a 12-volt test circuit. Fuses may become intermittent if they fatigue: when this happens they will conduct power until they get hot,

A basic tool roll, containing two crosshead and two flat-blade screwdrivers, seven combination spanners, cable ties, junior hacksaw and spare blades, baling wire, spare fasteners for the luggage rack, mole grips, pliers, Allen key to fit the rack fasteners, small chisel and electrical tape.

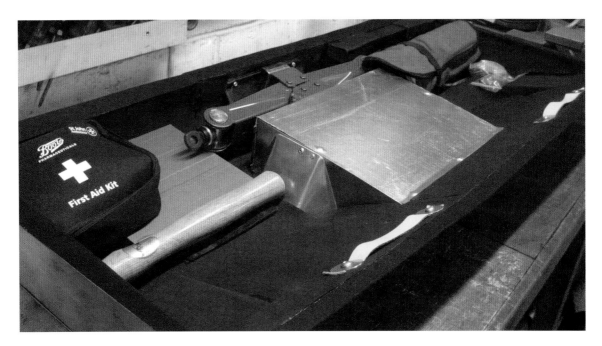

The aluminium section tool tray is packed as follows: from left to right: first aid kit, silver-covered wooden block for the jack, Thor hammer, scissor jack, square length of wood for use between hammer and wheelnuts, tool roll, and bag containing spare relays, fuses and test circuit.

when a hairline crack will open up and break the circuit. On cooling, current will flow again.

To deal with any bird droppings or tree sap, carry some liquid glass cleaner, a spray detailer, a water bottle, paper napkins, and a couple of microfibre cloths. Some bird droppings are very acidic, and if left for any time can etch into the paint and leave a mark that is difficult to remove later.

Cut a piece of wood in case you need to use your scissor jack in an emergency on soft ground. The size of the wood isn't so important, but it should be at least 200 x 200mm (8 x 8in), and it needs to be thick enough to take the weight of the Morgan on the jack, so at least 20mm (1in) thick. If the wood is wrapped in gaffer tape it will keep dry and wipe clean, should it be used in wet or muddy conditions.

Also pack a hi-vis waistcoat, which will slot under the seat, and a fold-away emergency triangle. I found one printed on a fabric square, which packs into a small wallet, and this also fits under the seat.

TYRE INFLATOR

Nothing creates discussion and generates opinion more than tyre inflator in an aerosol can. Most of what you hear or read about this product is not particularly good. Apparently it is not recommended – tyre fitters dislike it, the tyre must be replaced after using it, and so on. But many modern cars don't have a spare wheel, and come with a 12-volt compressor and a plastic bottle of inflator. More importantly, with a puncture on a cold wet night in a dangerous place, or even just in a dangerous place at any time, aerosol tyre inflator might just be good enough to allow the Morgan to be moved to a place of safety for changing the wheel.

An additional problem when touring is that having luggage on the rack is a further inconvenience when changing a wheel, and the rack itself is also an obstacle. Once the T bar is unscrewed, in most cases the luggage rack can be pivoted around the mounting brackets, or with some rack designs, just lifted away. However, lifting out the spare wheel with the rack still attached to the Morgan is not straightforward.

Removing the luggage rack completely makes this job much easier, but depending on the design of rack, you must carry the right-sized spanners – and don't lose the fasteners!

It is also essential to use your towels (or similar) under the luggage rack brackets to avoid damaging the rear panel when lifting it off – another reason for carrying those towels! And when replacing the spare wheel, unless you have adapted the spare-wheel well to support the wheel in the correct position, you may then also use the towels along the lower edge of the spare-wheel well, to hold the spare in position until the T bar is secured properly.

THE HALF-TONNEAU COVER

When out on the road, hood down and with luggage, the area behind the seats can be quite exposed, especially with the studded traditional hood, which removes completely. At Morgan events I have noticed that some owners will keep the studded hood attached along the rear panel, and will even sometimes leave it secured along the three turnbuckle fasteners on each side, with the hood folded as much as possible into the area behind the seats. This approach will certainly mean the hood can be raised much faster in the event of a sudden downpour, but it isn't a tidy solution.

A full tonneau cover will cover any luggage stowed in the area behind the seats, but the unused part of a full tonneau cover, plus the folded soft top, takes up quite a bit of space. To resolve this problem on our 4/4 Anniversary, which didn't have a full tonneau cover, I cut out a short but wide piece of mohair. I had this professionally edged, and used it to cover the area behind the seats, securing it with the fasteners on the body tub. At the front edge I adapted a fibreglass tent pole, which fitted between the soft top frames, at the pivots, to provide support, and this made an effective weatherproof tonneau cover for our luggage in that area.

The easy-up hood leaves an exposed area behind the seats across the rear of the car when folded, but the benefit of this hood design is that it adds up to 100mm (4in) of extra height to the area behind the

seats. In addition, the folded hood doesn't take up any space behind the seats, and so this increases the luggage capacity over that achieved with a studded hood. A hood cover on the easy-up hood does improve the look, and is very tidy when fitted.

The disadvantage of the hood cover is that because it fits under the rear catches and wraps around, and is secured with dura-dot fasteners, it takes practice to fit quickly. So in the event of a sudden shower, it can be difficult to remove quickly. Once removed, and with the hood raised, the hood cover then takes up space in the Morgan. In our early days of touring we would always use our hood cover, but more recently, and having been soaked a few times, I'm more content to travel without it when rain is forecast, even though the look is not so tidy!

LUGGAGE OPTIONS

We don't need to have our seats set fully back, so there is usable space between the seat backrest and the rear panel. The tilt/recline seats don't impinge on this area either when tilted forward to access behind the seats, so quite a few soft items will fit into this space. My usual items include the footpump, storm cover, the quick detailer and microfibres, the towels, and bottled drinking water. Hills Alive can supply two bespoke-shaped rear 'boxes' to fit in the space behind the seats above the tool tray, and some owners have made very good use of these.

We currently use soft bags, and even a suit bag will fit in the space, along with a normal selection of coats, hats and bagged-up shoes. At the outset, in 2008, we invested in the official Morgan luggage set from my local dealer. At that time, this was an American Tourister hard plastic suitcase with a black mohair cover, and black leather luggage straps. The mohair cover can be ordered in a colour to match your hood, and the leather luggage straps are also available in brown.

With this set comes a boot bag, which is a cylindrical duffle bag, also made from mohair. The boot bag has a robust half-zip running its full length, which zips on to the mohair cover of the suitcase, and the boot bag then travels on the luggage rack in front of

The Tourister suitcase with boot bag attached. The hood cover is in place, and the quarter tonneau cover fills the space between the cover and windstop. The boot bag rests on the high-level brake light, which over time can develop rub marks in the paintwork, unless protected.

the suitcase. However, in this position it rests on the Cobra high-level brake light, so I added a small neoprene cover, which rests on the Cobra and prevents abrasions. The boot bag also has a very convenient full-length zip opening, and has proved to be much more useful than the Tourister suitcase. It can be used as a stand-alone bag, and will either travel on the luggage rack or behind the seats.

As seasoned walkers (ramblers?) we have found that the boot bag is exactly the right size to carry all our walking gear, which includes boots, trousers,

waterproof trousers, socks, poles, maps and lightweight jackets. In fact this bag has become their permanent home and travels with us everywhere. I recently had to reproof it, because although mohair has a rubber inner lining, a long wet journey allowed water to penetrate the bag. On future wet journeys we will either wrap the contents, or the whole boot bag, in a bin liner, just to be safe.

The suitcase is huge and very well made. It is waterproof without the cover, and is more than big enough for the two of us. The disadvantage of this

The Over-Board bag with boot bag. Side straps hold the Over-Board bag securely, and the boot bag in place, but an eight-legged spider is an extra safety measure. If you begin your journey with the studded hood in place, leave room to store it when it is removed.

large suitcase is simply that when full, it is very heavy and difficult to handle on and off the luggage rack. It is also quite difficult to fit and remove the mohair cover, and this cover isn't a particularly good fit around the end of the case with wheels. When lifted off the luggage rack, and with the mohair cover removed, the case wheels make it quite easy to move about.

I've considered using this suitcase as an external boot, by putting other soft bags inside it, but so far we haven't tried this approach. Some owners do something very similar, by obtaining a large old suit-

case, which they bolt on to the luggage rack for the duration of their trip, and use it as an external boot. Hill Alive can also supply a 'MogBox', a wedge-shaped lockable box that fixes on to the luggage rack as an external boot.

Given the limitations of the Tourister suitcase, we have looked at other options, and eventually arrived on the website of Over-Board. This is a modern company that specializes in waterproof bags for most applications, even down to small bags for mobile phone protection. I measured the width of the luggage rack, and obtained a cylindrical duffel-type bag that fits across the rack exactly. This product has adjustable end straps, and will therefore secure to the rack without any additional fasteners. To be on the safe side I usually also use an elasticated spider, with the conventional eight-legged arrangement with a hook on each leg; these are widely available on-line.

The Over-Board bag doesn't have a zip, but closes with a double wrap-over arrangement that secures with Velcro. We have tested this bag to the limit on long wet drives, and it has remained totally dry inside. Furthermore, it holds almost as much as the Tourister suitcase, but is much easier to handle between us, with a handle at each end. Apparently it will float when dropped into deep water, but so far we haven't tested this feature.

THE SAT-NAV

We rarely use a sat-nav, much preferring to navigate a pre-prepared route from a map using tulip contour graphics. For the odd occasion when we do use a sat-nav, I have added a circular plastic mount to the left corner of the dashboard, secured with double-sided tape. I have covered this mount with a black leather circle when it is not in use. The leather has a circle of soft clear plastic stuck to the back, and this holds it to the mount satisfactorily.

The built-in 12-volt feed for accessories is usually located in the glove compartment, or under the dashboard in the plastic finishing panel. Adaptors are available on-line that provide two 12-volt outlets, and some also have USB ports. The portable battery pack

Finally, what it's all about: a Morgan and the open road. Scotland in May 2014.

mentioned earlier can also be used to power accessories independently of the vehicle electrical system. Any items such as this mount which are attached with double-sided tape, may be removed easily using dental floss in a sawing motion. The residue can then be removed using white spirit, without damaging the surface.

POST TOURING TASKS

A week or two on the road does have an effect on a Morgan. On a good weather trip there will at least be a covering of flies, while on a touring holiday where there is wet weather, then most aspects of the car will need attention on returning home. There are commercially available insect-removing sprays, and these work well. I rarely wash my Morgan, preferring to use 'quick detailer', but when I do use a bucket and water, I cover the engine with a bin liner to keep it dry. Leave a note on the steering wheel to remind you to remove it! I build up the polish on the bodywork slowly with two or three applications, starting with quick detailer, which is a clear liquid, and taking care that the microfibre cloths are clean, and free of grit.

For the interior, I remove the front carpet mats and do a full vacuum to lift the dust and 'white bits'. I also check for wet patches, but am confident that my dehumidifier will sort this out over a few days. If the leather is looking a bit tired, I will apply leather cleaner and conditioner. My favourite, from Turtle Wax, was recently rebranded, and has lost the delightful smell it used to have.

Use glass cleaner on the windscreen and sidescreen windows, carefully in the case of the sidescreens, to avoid scratching. Check all the chafing points around the doors and bonnets, and reapply the neoprene or leather buffers as necessary.

I leave the wire wheels until last, and usually start at the rear. I lift the rear end, make it safe, and then first do the inside of the wheels and tyres, using quick detailer, or in the case of heavy soiling on the rims, WD40 or white spirit. With a bit of effort, the backs of the wheels can be cleaned very successfully using this approach, including the brake drums.

Next I do the outside of the wheels, again using quick detailer, and agitating around the spokes with a paintbrush. I use a microfibre cloth to polish up. Stainless wire wheels are much easier to clean than those finished in black! Whilst the rear is in the air, I wipe down the exhaust with an old rag and WD40. This is to prevent a build-up of grime. I also give the underside a visual check, looking for damage or leaks, and remove any stones from the tyre treads, and apply tyre dressing to the outside and the inside of the tyres.

Next I lift the front, and apply the same approach. In this case the wheels can be put on lock, so access is much easier. Now it is time to pump some grease into the stub axles. The top nipples are usually temperamental, and this is because the grease galleries are tiny, and so it takes a bit of practice to get the grease in the nipple, and not everywhere else. The lower grease nipples, which are the important ones, are much more cooperative, and after five or six strokes, the grease will emerge from around the steering bearings. Finally a wipe over, so that none migrates on to the brake discs.

After a bad weather tour, I also remove the luggage rack and spare wheel. It doesn't usually take long to bring the shine back to the spare, and I visually check inside the spare-wheel well for leaks.

And so after a day and a half of effort, and taking care of things, I can stand back and admire a perfectly clean Morgan. Until the next time.

SPECIALIST WEBSITES

I have found the following companies, specialists and on-line resources extremely useful over the years. I have not listed the current Morgan dealers here, because current information about the dealer network is available on the Morgan Motor Co. website. The dealer network has always evolved over time, and will continue to do so. At the time of writing, this list will provide much of what you may need as an owner and enthusiast of the modern traditional Morgan in the UK. It is not meant to be exhaustive, however, so please accept my apologies if I have omitted your favourite supplier or website! There are Morgan specialists in most overseas markets where Morgans are sold, especially in Europe and the United States.

The Morgan Motor Company: For new cars, car creator, car locator, dealer locator, factory tours, on-line shop, and Company news feed. Look for the current full worldwide dealer list.
www.morgan-motor.co.uk

The Morgan Sports Car Club:
www.morgansportscarclub.com

Talk Morgan: The Britannica of Morgan on-line discussion.
www.talkmorgan.com

Morganatica: An on-line workshop manual.
sites.google.com/site/morganatica/home

GoMog: The original on-line Morgan workshop manual.
www.gomog.com

Heart of England Morgans (John Worrall): Very extensive range of stainless-steel and other accessories. The original stainless-steel chassis cross-member covers.
www.heartofenglandmorgans.co.uk

Hillsalive: Bespoke Luggage Solutions
www.hillsalive.co.uk

Librands (Rob Wells): Extensive range of accessories, including the acclaimed stainless door checks.
www.librands.co.uk

Luigi Borghi: Bespoke Morgan dashboards and accessories.
www.borghiautomobili.it

MK Holztechnik (Matthias Kauffelt): Bespoke Morgan dashboards and accessories.
www.mk-holztechnik.de

Morgan Car Badges (Hermen Pol):
www.morgancarbadges.com

Morganville: Home of the Morgan Registry.
www.morganville.org

Mulfab (Peter Mulberry): Steering and suspension, radiators, modified roadster sumps.
www.mulfab.co.uk

MWS: Motor Wheel Service: Wire wheel specialist and supplier to Morgan Motor Co.
www.mwsint.com

New Elms (Tim Ayres): Workshop, Rutherford modified suspension.
www.newelms.com

Over-Board: Waterproof luggage.
www.over-board.co.uk

Phoenix Design (John Taylor): Hood frame swivel pivots, storm covers, cockpit covers, door mirrors, bonnet extensions.
www.morganhoods.com

SiFab (Simon Hall): Aluminium radiators, engineering and fabrication solutions.
www.sifab.co.uk

V.S.M. Malvern Ltd: Ash frames, steel and aluminium wings, bonnets.
www.morganspecialist.com

Wolf Performance (Cain Poulton): Specialist performance accessories.
www.wolfperformance.co.uk

MATERIALS

The following list is of companies from which I have had good service over the past eight years of Morgan 'improvements'.

Agriemach: Heat and sound insulation.
www.agriemach.com

C.O.H. Baines: Neoprene profile.
www.coh-baines.co.uk

Holden Vintage & Classic:
www.holden.co.uk

Namrick: Nut and bolt store.
www.namrick.co.uk

Perspex Sheet:
Sheet Plastics: www.sheetplastics.co.uk
The Plastic Man: www.theplasticman.co.uk
R.H. Nuttall Ltd: Neoprene sheets.
www.rhnuttall.co.uk

Woolies: Trim, upholstery and fittings.
www.woolies-trim.co.uk

Leather: The best source of leather offcuts seems to be eBay. It is worth contacting the supplier to establish the thickness of the leather required, because thin leather is much easier to work with, but is harder to source, because it is less common. However, dealers with trimming facilities will also have offcuts, so it may be worth asking the question.

THE DEALER NOTICE FROM 1997

MORGAN

MORGAN MOTOR

COMPANY LTD.

REGISTERED IN LONDON UNDER NO. 971255
Directors: P. H. G. Morgan, J. D. Morgan
C. P. H. Morgan, D. J. Day, M. G. Owen
H. M. Morgan
Secretary: G. M. Margetts

Our ref   Your ref

TELEPHONE
01684 573104

FAX NUMBER: 01684 892295

BUILDERS OF THE MORGAN SPORTS CAR

REGISTERED OFFICE

PICKERSLEIGH ROAD
MALVERN LINK
WORCS. WR14 2LL ENGLAND

DEALER NOTICE

JUNE 1997 BODY WORK REVISIONS:

As you will be aware, the new price increase recently circulated covers the costs related to the biggest number of changes to the car since the 1950's. We have listed here the main alterations the components which may be of assistance.

Body Frame

Virtually every part of the wooden frame has been altered. The doors have been moved back around 25mm in the body and the shape has been changed. The top of the door has been lengthened more than the bottom. The hinge positions have changes as has the rear angle and top sweep. As a result the elbow rail, rocker and hinge pillars have all changed. The wheel arches have been reduced in width by 25mm each side and so the sill board has changed. The corners of the top rear frame have been filled in to give a sweep from the top of the wheel arch into the top of the rear panel. The rear inside frame and spare wheel frame have both been changed. The dash board has been set back into the scuttle be 75mm and the angle has seen made more upright. All the parts of the dash and scuttle have changed.

This obviously means that all the Body panels and Trim work will change. None of these parts are interchangeable with the current cars. Aluminium doors are now standard, as are aluminium bonnets.

The Hood frame on 2 -str and the shape of the hood have also changed. The tonneau will change as will arm rests and arm rest bars. The crash padding rubber and trim will be the same. Glove box and mounting will all change.

A new specification scuttle roll bar will be used and fitted as standard. this is lower than before to allow clearance for the new dash position and has a step for the column.

Side screens

The side screens are all new. The channel used has been changed to increase the radius to conform to new regulations. The dimensions have been changed to match the revised door, they are around 60mm longer. The mounting bars and trim panel have been altered .

On the 4-str the rear side screens have been reduced and will no longer be designed to slide. The front have been modified in line with the 2-str.

JUNE 1997 BODY WORK REVISIONS:

Dash Board

The layout of the dash has been changes to allow for the new steering column and position in the scuttle. The main dials and warning lights are now mounted in a steel panel in front of the driver. The switches are in two blocks, one each side of the main dial panel, set into the wood, in blocks of 3. The small dials are in a group of 4 in the middle of the panel. The dash board rheostat is included in the switch blocks and the switches are of the same size as before, but with a new design of rocker. The switches have been turned through 90 deg. and new light symbols are used because of this

The switches will be:

Front Spot Lights	Heater Blower
Rear Fog Lights	Electrically Heated Windscreen
Dash Light Rheostat	Hazard Warning Lights

The lights will now be controlled from the left hand column stalk, by a rotary control from Off at the bottom, then Side Lights and then Headlights. The dip is by a 'Click - on, Click - Off' pull of the stalk. The indicators are operated from this stalk by pushing up or down.

The wipers are operated by the right hand stalk, again a rotary control. Off at the bottom, Intermittent next, then First speed and then Second. The intermittent is variable, controlled by a rotary restate on the stalk. Fast is about 4 seconds, slow is about 10. The washer is operated by pulling the stalk toward the wheel and the wipers will automatically operate 4 times. The stalk can be pushed downward for a single wipe.

The horn will now be in the centre of the new specification steering wheel.

There will only be one specification of dash board for 2 and 4 stator and these will be available in walnut veneer as an option.

Steering Wheel/Column

The steering wheel will be changed along with the mounting boss, column, column mounting and UJ shaft. The new wheel will be similar to the current and available in 15" (standard) and 14" optional. The centre spokes will be covered completely with a rubber cover with a horn push under the centre. This cover, along with the new mounting boss is all part of the new crash test standard. The new column will be mounted to the metal front by aluminium brackets top and bottom. This is also part of the revisions for the tests. The spline for mounting the wheel boss is different to that on the current unit.

The column has a downward height adjustment operated by a lever on the left of the column top cover.
Page 2:

JUNE 1997 BODY WORK REVISIONS:

Steering Wheel/Column

The nut for the column/ wheel boss has been changed to match the thread on the new column.There is a new column top cover and the ignition lock is in this cover on the right of the column. This cover fits around the indicator/wiper stalks in two halves.

The UJ shaft on the Plus8 and Plus 4 will change to the one currently used on the 4/4. The 4/4 has a new shorter unit to allow for the longer column. The drivers side wing valance has been altered to allow for the new steering position. The rubber block on the new UJ shafts will be at the bottom of the shaft.

Windscreen/Heater

Because of the new position of the dash board , there is no longer room behind for the de mister vents. This has meant a change to the heater to remove the de mister outlets, which have been replaced with round directional vents to help air flow in the car.

The windscreen will now be fitted with electric heating elements as seen on may new cars. These will now be used as the de-mist system. The screen will be operated by a switch on the dash board. As this is the de-mist, it will not have a timer, as it may have to be used continuously.

Seats

The basic specification of seat will remain the same, but a new type runner will be used. This has a broader base for better stability and a new runner release system. In place of the lever under the seat, a bar is fitted just ahead of the front cushion , which is pulled up to move the seat . An anti submarine plate has been fitted to the standard bucket seat and the recliner, for use with the air bag system in the USA.

Air Bag System

The air bag system offered is of the Mechanical type, not electrically triggered. The bags are activated by a large frontal impact, the force is transferred to the wheel or passenger bag unit and this fires the bag. The specification used has been specially developed for the Morgan and no part is interchangeable with other systems. It is most important to note that, unless the air bag has been disabled, Child seats must not be fitted in cars equipped with Air Bag systems. If an air bag car is to be worked on, there is a special pin available to lock the system mechanically. The force required to set the bag of is very high, but care must be taken. A special scuttle bar is used for air bag cars, along with a different dash and certain other special parts.

Full Details of the air bag set-up will be supplied with each car and to the dealers.

Page 3

JUNE 1997 BODY WORK REVISIONS:

4.6 litre Plus 8

As it has not been possible to obtain the current Range Rover 4.6 litre engine, due to supply problems within Rover and because of the modifications required for installation, we have arranged for a special engine to be prepared.

This uses the current 3.9 litre engine, but built using the standard 4.6 litre block. This involves stripping a new engine, removing the block, specially modifying a 4.6 block to accept the front cover and rebuilding the engine. This produces a special unit using largely standard Rover parts. The distributor set-up is the same as 3.9, as is the cam shaft and ECU. The block is cross bolted for strength. The crank, pistons and block are standard Range Rover 4.6.

Capacity: 4555cc

Bore/Stroke: 94/82 mm

Power: 220 BHP (164KW) @ 5000 rpm

Torque: 260 lb/ft (353 Nm) @ 3600 rpm

Bumpers

The new car will be fitted with Polished Stainless Steel bumpers, these will be of the same design as the current chrome bumper at present. Later the end will be filled in as part of the safety modification.

The rest of the car specification remains the same at present.

Specification Changes from June 1997

+8, +4 & 4/4

~ Curved body shape with better hood line.

~ Long door for better access.

~ Wheel arches 2" wider apart for more rearward seat adjustment and extra width in the luggage area.

~ Dashboard moved forward to allow for dished steering wheel on air bag models.

~ Glove box better size.

~ New direction and light switches and wiper control switch with delay. Switches much better quality.

~ Horn in centre of wheel for ease of use.

~ Steering wheel adjustable (up and down) by 15 degrees.

~ Double lock seat runners set wider apart - to prevent rattling when not occupied.

~ Seats lowered and angled to slope front to rear to allow more room for taller drivers. Also improves headroom and visibility through the sidescreens.

~ Battery moved to right hand side to improve balance of car (especially LHD).

~ Electric heated windscreen.

~ Stainless steel exhaust on all cars.

~ Internal roll bar in stainless steel as standard!

+8 & 4/4

~   Axle ratios changed to ensure cars meet EEC noise regulations:-

4/4   3.73 ÷ 1
+8   3.23 ÷ 1

~   1st gear is now a sensible ratio - especially on 4.6 litre when extra 20% of torque compensates for ratio change.

~   All cars now easier to adapt from right to left hand drive.

~   Stainless steel fuel pipes.

~   Fuel pump integral inside tank (no jams/leakages).

~   Instruments - trip setting.

Airbag Test Results
Bill Beck 2.30pm

The Morgan Motor Company is the first small manufacturer to develop a full airbag system which is available to everyone.

Morgan uses latest de-powered airbags which go off gently and have never resulted in a death - unlike the old American versions.

Morgan achieved the best results MIRA have ever seen in a frontal impact test due to:-

~   Good car design.
~   Long bonnet.
~   Wood frame dissipates shock.
~   Car collapses progressively.

Noise Tests

~   All cars passed tests easily.

~   Stainless steel exhaust system sounds and looks good.

~   Car is more pleasant to drive on long journeys.

~   Environmentally friendly.

BIBLIOGRAPHY

Hensing, Andreas/Otte, Dagmar *Making a Morgan* (Veloce Publishing Ltd)

Morgan, Charles/Houston Bowden, Gregory *Morgan: 100 Years – The Official History Of The Worlds Greatest Sports Car* (Michael O'Mara Books Ltd)

Palmer, Michael *Morgan 4/4, The First Seventy-Five Years* (The Crowood Press Ltd)

Scarlett, Michael *Morgan Plus 8* (Haynes Publishing Ltd)

Worrall, John/Turner, Liz *Original Morgan 4/4, Plus 4 and Plus 8* (Bay View Books Ltd)

Morgan Motor Company: copies of *The Owner's Handbook*

Morgan Motor Company website, and sales brochures 1997–2017

INDEX